WHAT MANNER OF LOVE

Raymond H. Woolsey

REVIEW AND HERALD® PUBLISHING ASSOCIATION
HAGERSTOWN, MD 21740

The author assumes full responsibility for the accuracy of all facts and quotations as cited in this book.

Unless otherwise noted, all biblical references are from The New King James Version. Copyright © 1979, 1980, 1982, Thomas Nelson, Inc., Publishers.

Texts credited to NEB are from *The New English Bible*. © The Delegates of the Oxford University Press and the Syndics of the Cambridge University Press 1961, 1970. Reprinted by permission.

Texts credited to NIV are from the *Holy Bible, New International Version*. Copyright © 1973, 1978, 1984, International Bible Society. Used by permission of Zondervan Bible Publishers.

This book was
Edited by Richard W. Coffen
Designed by Patricia S. Wegh
Cover design by Mark O'Connor
Typeset: 11/12 Times

PRINTED IN U.S.A.

99 98 97 96 95   5 4 3 2 1

Library of Congress Cataloging in Publication Data
Woolsey, Raymond H.
     What manner of love / Raymond H. Woolsey.
          p.   cm.
     1. Salvation. 2. Grace (Theology) 3. Seventh-day Adventists—Doctrines.
I. Title.
     BT751.2.W66   1995
     234—dc20   94-46262
                                                                CIP

ISBN 0-8280-0932-5

WHAT MANNER OF LOVE

Dedication

To the members of my Sabbath school class
at Willow Brook church, Boonsboro, Maryland.
You inspire me to dig deeply into the mine of truth.

Contents

God Tries to Get Through

1

The use of words as symbols comes naturally to human beings. "Seashore." "Jungle." "Traffic." Just speak or read the words, and certain scenes come to your mind. "Angry." "Serene." "Happy." Even emotions stir within us simply from seeing certain letters printed on paper. And not only human beings but also pets, dolphins, and apes can learn the meaning of spoken or displayed words and react correspondingly.

But there must be some background, some previous experience, for the word-symbol to work. When you come across a word you've never met before, it evokes no image.

Similarly to the spoken or written word, certain people become symbols to us. Even a stranger may evoke an emotion or attitude, again depending on our past experience and connotation. When you see a dirty, disheveled person with shifty eyes and glowering expression, you feel dread and distaste. Your reactions to "mother" and "father" will depend on the kind of childhood you had.

God uses this predisposition on our part to employ symbols to help us know Him. He wants us to understand His character, to know and appreciate His attitude toward us. He wants us to be aware of the danger we are in because of our sinful condition, and He wants us to know that help is available. So He uses words—the Word, the Bible—to communicate between His mind and our minds.

But words are not always sufficient for communication. To a person who has been born blind, some words are useless. Try to explain to such a person the meaning of "red" or "shiny." Even among people with sight, some things are best expressed in other ways than with words. Gestures, voice tone, deeds—these all serve as avenues for communicating ideas and attitudes.

God also finds the written word insufficient for revealing Himself to us. And so He became a human being like us, living with us, sharing our experiences, but always demonstrating God's character, God's purpose.

Jesus the God-man is a symbol of God's caring nature. In all the vastness of space (with its myriads of island universes) take one small galaxy, the Milky Way. From that whirling cluster of stars (most hundreds of thousands of light-years apart) select a medium-sized sun. Single out a planet of that sun. Here it is— Earth, the one rebellious speck in all of God's heavens. Though most do not know it, the people of that Earth are headed to oblivion because of their rebellion.

God seeks to rescue those people. He lays aside His majesty, His omnipotence, His omniscience, to become a human being, one of millions, on that planet. Then, still in the process of rescue, this God-man accepts vilification and death at the hands of other human beings. Yes, in Himself Jesus symbolizes the length and breadth, the height and depth, of God's love.

But Jesus is more than a symbol. In Him is the force; He is the dynamic (Greek *dynamis,* from which we get the word "dynamite") that accomplishes what God's love calls for in the wayward human race.

It is important at the outset of this book that we understand the meaning of terms. Take the word "sin," for example. Many people see the word as referring to wrong deeds, actions that God does not like. In their thinking, one can count up the number of times one has done something "against the Ten Commandments." If they can recognize or remember those times and be forgiven of God for each one, then they are OK. They are "savable."

But sin is more than an act. It is an attitude; it is a state of rebellion against God. Lucifer sinned in heaven when he refused to have God as his Lord. Eve sinned even before her first bite of forbidden fruit. Her sin was in thinking that God did not really have her best good at heart, that she could do better fending for herself. Adam sinned when he took the attitude that momentary self-indulgence was more important than putting God first.

Each set self above God. Call it pride, call it selfishness—it is all the same. It was that spirit which Satan sought to engender in Jesus during the wilderness temptations. The suggestion that Jesus turn stones into bread carried the inference that He show what *He* could do. (Remember that Jesus had left His divine prerogatives behind when He became a human being. He was to face life as the rest of the human race did.) The urging that Jesus jump off the Temple was a dare that Jesus demand God to save Him. And, of course, the promise to give Jesus the kingdoms of the world if He would acknowledge Satan as ruler of this planet was a blatant challenge that Jesus think of what would be *easy for Him* rather than what love would do.

Self rather than God. That is what Satan chose and what he has always been trying to get others of God's creatures to choose. When we recognize God as the only source of life, it is easy to understand why rebellion against Him means death. It is not just an arbitrary sentence handed down by the Judge of the universe (though God does actively effect it); it is the natural consequence of our choice(s).

But for us poor human beings, it is in our very nature to look to ourselves. When we set up gods, we clothe them with characteristics such as our own. Even when we recognize our sinfulness, in our insufferable pride we feel that we are the ones to do something about it. We feel that we can improve ourselves, remove our guilt, lift ourselves by our own bootstraps. But we can no more change our self-directed attention than we can change the fact that we are human beings. Our nature is selfish; we are sinful from the inside out.

So God steps in to do what we cannot do for ourselves. He doesn't just help us straighten up our act; He changes the kind of person we are; He reaches in and re-creates our psyche, our innermost being. We are a "new creation" (see 2 Cor. 5:17), with a new nature.

Although God Himself does not change, He is the master of change. He took this world when it was a shapeless glob and transformed it into a garden of beauty. When humankind rebelled against God's plan, becoming so depraved it could hardly live with itself, God sent the Flood and altered the world so much that scientists are still trying to figure it out. Then God sent His Son to walk among us, and the world has never been the same since.

Nor is God finished with His work of change. Although this world will "grow old like a garment" (Ps. 102:26), when Jesus comes the third time, our planet will be made new—"rebuilt at the factory," if you will. And God will populate the new world with the people He has made new.

Why does God do all this? Why does He bother? Ah, that is the question! Just as it is our fallen human nature to rebel, so it is God's nature to love. He loves this world as much as He loves all the other worlds and other creatures He has made. And He loves all of us on earth, regardless of our attitude toward Him. His love is the same; it is only our response that varies.

Jesus loves every sinner and all sinners. And He loves us in our sin, *while we are sinning.* "God demonstrates His own love toward us, in that while we were still sinners, Christ died for us" (Rom. 5:8). That is the way it would have to be. God cannot wait until we have cleaned up our act before He loves us, because without Him we cannot clean up our act. If He is going to help us at all, it must be while we are rebellious, repulsive, wicked.

That is why the word "grace" comes into the picture. In its simplest form, grace means love. But human beings have loaded the word "love" with so much baggage that it has almost lost meaning. We use the word for our pets, for our favorite television programs, for the gewgaws and gimcracks we find in souvenir stores. We even use when we mean "lust."

But God's love for us is different. He loves us when we are unlovable. He loves us even though we have done nothing to earn it; we do not merit it or deserve it. He loves us whether or not we love Him in return.

In music a "grace note" is a note or phrase that is added to decorate the composition. It is not necessary to the musical theme; the piece would be whole without it. But the composer (or the performer) has added it for an extra bit of pleasure. So God does not *have* to love us. He would be perfectly within His rights to let us reap the consequences of our sin. But His love goes beyond that.

The serious word student might be interested in the following (abstracted from Marvin R. Vincent, *Word Studies in the New*

12

Testament, vol. 1, pp. 259, 260): The word "grace" is used to translate the Greek word *charis* (pronounced with a hard *k),* from the root word *chairein,* "to rejoice" (the same root from which we get the word "charisma"). The primary meaning of the word is "that which gives joy or pleasure." Scriptural connotations include "a beautiful or agreeable sentiment felt and expressed toward another; kindness, favor, good-will." It refers to "the higher Christian signification, based on the emphasis of *freeness* in the gift or favor, . . . spontaneous, absolute loving-kindness of God toward men, and so contrasted with *debt, law, works, sin."*

Another way of looking at grace is "love in action." God's love toward us is not passive. He doesn't just sit back and say, "I love you all. Whenever you feel like it, you can come to Me and I will accept you." No, His love is active; it goes out and does things. God says, "Yes, I have loved you with an everlasting love; therefore with lovingkindness I have drawn you" (Jer. 31:3). Jesus paints the picture more succinctly: "I, if I am lifted up from the earth [referring to His crucifixion], will draw all peoples to Myself" (John 12:32).

That is why we speak and sing of "amazing grace." "Grace is amazing because it works against the grain of common sense. Hard-nosed common sense will tell you that you are too wrong to meet the standards of a holy God; pardoning grace tells you that it's all right in spite of so much in you that is wrong.

"Realistic common sense tells you that you are too weak, too harassed, too human to change for the better; grace gives you power to send you on the way to being a better person.

"Plain common sense may tell you that you are caught in a rut of fate or futility; grace promises that you can trust God to have a better tomorrow for you than the day you have made for yourself" (Lewis Smedes, *How Can It Be All Right When Everything Is All Wrong?* pp. 9, 10).

John Newton knew whereof he wrote when he penned the words to the beloved song "Amazing Grace." For years Newton captained a slave ship, dealing in the barter of human flesh. So inured was he to the ramifications of his trade that he never had "the least scruple as to its lawfulness." But Newton was converted and married a Christian woman. He studied for the ministry and became a zealous preacher and faithful pastor.

Then Newton could look back on his life and the patience God had exercised in his behalf:

"Amazing grace! how sweet the sound,
   that saved a wretch like me!
I once was lost, but now am found,
   Was blind, but now I see."

But was Newton so much more of a wretch than any of us? Was his slave trading more odious than our self-centeredness? Remember, God does not weigh the deed—rather, He measures the extent of our rebellion against Him. It is in this sense that Ellen White could write: "We think with horror of the cannibal who feasts on the still warm and trembling flesh of his victim; but are the results of even this practice more terrible than are the agony and ruin caused by misrepresenting motive, blackening reputation, dissecting character?" *(Education,* p. 235).

Verily, we are all sinners, standing in the need of grace.

"By grace you have been saved through faith, and that not of yourselves; it is the gift of God" (Eph. 2:8). Notice that it is not our faith which saves us. Salvation is by Jesus' death in our place, the outworking of God's grace. Faith is the instrument, the avenue, by which we access grace. Both the faith and the grace are God's gifts.

Divine grace did not stop with the death of Jesus on the cross. That sacrifice atoned for our sins—it expunged our record of guilt. But more is needed. Since it is our fallen nature to sin, then just clearing up our past is not enough. Our nature has to be changed.

The change that God makes in men and women is at the heart of His plan of salvation. The Bible uses various metaphors to describe this transition. Jesus called it being "born again." Paul used the sense of "adoption" into the family of God. To Ezekiel, God used the metaphor of exchanging a heart of flesh for our heart of stone. It is, essentially, our conversion, to use another metaphor. The Holy Spirit impresses upon us our sinfulness, and in deep contrition we repent of the rebellion that alienated us from God.

Being "dead to sin" (another metaphor, preparatory to the "new birth"), we are ready for the Holy Spirit, as Christ's personal representative, to set up residence in our hearts. As we yield our wills into His control (just as Jesus did when He was on earth) He reshapes our characters. With our attention on Jesus and His holiness, His obedience, His joy, His oneness with the Father, the Spirit little by little—to the extent we surrender ourselves—molds our lives, our nature, to be like Jesus.

This is love at work. God loves us, and we respond with love to Him and He draws us to Himself. Notice how essential here is a knowledge of Jesus. That is why we have not one but four accounts of His life on earth. Not only did Jesus die for us, redeeming us from sin's curse, but He lived a life of joyful obedience. His life on earth accomplished several things: (1) It proved that God really loves us, that He should so condescend to live with us, as one of us; (2) it proved Satan wrong in his claim that God's principles of government are bankrupt, that it is impossible to obey Him; (3) it provided us an example—the example—of how we may live through His enabling power.

Jesus is the living embodiment of God's principles, an ongoing demonstration of His love. To one who has experienced Him, Jesus is a symbol of God's direct involvement with the human race. He is love personified, grace incarnate.

The very mention of His name evokes joy.

Jesus!

The
Eloquent Prophet

2

Suppose you have been asked to serve on a committee to nomi-
nate a new president for your local conference. One of the first
things you will want to do, along with your fellow committee
members, is to ascertain what qualities you will look for in a candidate. You will no doubt list those qualities and prioritize them.

For example, you will want someone who is a good administra-
tor, but who also has a pastoral attitude. The candidate should have
a feel for financial matters, yet possess a zeal for evangelism, for
growth. You will probably hope for a president who is good at detail and at the same time has great vision as to what can be. And the
individual should be able to inspire others toward the same vision.

Realistically, you know you probably will not find all the
qualifications in the same person, but you will seek until you find
someone with the most important ones. Your list will guide you in
that search.

Of course, the "position" of Messiah was not a matter of elec-
tion, and neither would human option play a role in determining His
qualifications. But a detailed description of the Messiah's attributes,
personality, strengths, and methods would go a long way in preparing people for His appearance. This would help in identifying Him
when He came and also in readying hearts for His mission.

Beginning with Adam and Eve and through the millennia that
followed, God shared with His people hints and tips, bits and
pieces, of the divine initiative. These served to keep hope alive;
they reminded them that God had not forsaken His promise. But

they did not convey much information as to the nature and work of the awaited One.

Then we come to Isaiah, who lays it all out. Not only did he reveal to the people of his time what the Messiah would be like, but writers of the New Testament continued to search his prophecies for insights into the mysteries of divine grace. More than 90 times they quoted from him. And still today we depend heavily on Isaiah, the "gospel prophet," for the underpinnings of our faith.

Isaiah was born into the royal family of Judah, although not in line for kingship. His career spanned 60 years, from 745 B.C. to the accession of the evil King Manasseh. Four kings sat on the throne of Judah during Isaiah's long ministry—Uzziah, Jotham, Ahaz, and Hezekiah.

It was a time of prosperity for both Judah and the kingdom of Israel to the north. But it was also a time of great moral and political danger. Long before, the 10 northern tribes had set a course of idolatry and rebellion. Each successive king proved to be more evil than his predecessor. Now the nation was in a nosedive to disaster. Isaiah witnessed the invasions by the powerful Assyrian armies, the horrible decimation of the kingdom of Israel, the forced removal of practically all the population.

In turn, the Assyrian hordes raided Judah and even surrounded Jerusalem. The powerful preaching of Isaiah, the prophet-statesman, helped Judah escape, for a time, Israel's fate. Fearlessly he assailed king and populace, calling attention to their need for repentance and reformation. And always he tempered his sermons with hope and promise.

Jewish scholars considered Isaiah as the greatest of prophets—his book leads the books of the Prophets, which along with the Law and the Writings make up the Jewish holy canon. His diction is recognized as the best in Hebrew literature.

Christian students also recognize Isaiah as a preeminent author. "Different writers speak of the lofty and majestic calmness, the energy and liveliness, of the style of Isaiah. He is called an expert in the use of images, of epigrams and metaphors. His descriptions are vivid with a wonderful variety of style. His Hebrew is of the purest and best, his vocabulary larger than that of any other book of the Bible" (M. L. Andreasen, *Isaiah, the Gospel Prophet*, p. 9).

In view of his education, dauntlessness, and erudition, Isaiah has been called the Old Testament's Saul of Tarsus. Like that later messenger, Isaiah also saw a vision of God in heaven (see chapter 6), and God entrusted him with the mission of revealing Himself to His people.

About 10 years after Isaiah's divine call, the great Tiglath-pileser III made threatening moves against Syria, Israel, and Judah. When Ahaz, who had followed his father, Jotham, to Judah's throne, seemed ready to ally himself with the Assyrians, the other two kings prepared to take him out. At this juncture, Isaiah appeared to his king with the Lord's promise to be with him if he refrained from entangling alliances.

God would give Ahaz a sign, Isaiah said, to signify the surety of His promise: "Behold, the virgin shall conceive and bear a Son, and shall call His name Immanuel. Curds and honey He shall eat, that He may know to refuse the evil and choose the good. For before the Child shall know to refuse the evil and choose the good, the land that you dread will be forsaken by both her kings" (Isa. 7:14-16).

The version quoted here, The New King James, makes this passage a reference (through the use of capital letters) to the virgin Mary and the birth of Jesus. But the original Hebrew is not so clear-cut. The Hebrew 'almah means "young woman," without reference to virginity. By contrast, Isaiah could have used bethulah, which would have specified a woman without sexual experience.

Obviously, Isaiah referred to a conception and birth that would take place in the near future. Otherwise, it would not be effective as a sign to Ahaz. Yet Isaiah must have also recognized another, more portentous, meaning to his own words.

We interrupt ourselves here to note that on many occasions prophets gave messages that held double, or if you will, "bifocal" meaning. One was contemporary, with reference to the immediate circumstances; the other looked to the future for application and fulfillment. The statement to the serpent in Eden about the bruising of heads and heels was such a prophecy. In a promise made to David, he understood the reference to his "seed" as applying to his immediate son and also to the Messiah.

This double application was certainly true of Isaiah's prophecy. Matthew points out clearly that the virgin birth of Jesus was in direct fulfillment of Isaiah's promise to Ahaz (see Matt. 1:22, 23).

Sometimes the prophets themselves did not fully comprehend the duality of their message. Though they may have had an inkling of its import, not always did they understand the implications. Thus we read, "Of this salvation the prophets have inquired and searched diligently, who prophesied of the grace that would come to you, searching what, or what manner of time, the Spirit of Christ who was in them was indicating when He testified beforehand the sufferings of Christ and the glories that would follow. To them it was revealed that, not to themselves, but to us they were ministering the things which now have been reported to you through those who have preached the gospel to you by the Holy Spirit sent from heaven—things which angels desire to look into" (1 Peter 1:10-12).

But Isaiah must have sensed that the Holy Spirit had spoken through him of the coming of the Lord. "Immanuel" was more than just a name for a baby—it was a statement: "God with us!" Only 36 verses later Isaiah broke into exultation: "For unto us a Child is born, unto us a Son is given; and the government will be upon His shoulder. And His name shall be called Wonderful, Counselor, Mighty God, Everlasting Father, Prince of Peace" (Isa. 9:6).

No equivocation here, no dual speech. In soaring expression unsurpassed in the Bible, with unexcelled depth of feeling and words of beauty, Isaiah proclaimed the most stupendous news: very God will become very Man.

Regardless of how Isaiah comprehended his own words, for us there can be no room for misunderstanding. Here is the promise, not of one who would represent God, or one sent from God, but the mighty God Himself, who would forsake His celestial throne, His cosmic majesty, to join the human scene.

"Unto us a Child is born, unto us a Son is given." Born of a woman, part and parcel of the human race, one of us, one *with* us—partaking of our same nature, sharing our same concerns. No one had so much as dreamed it before. Other religions have their humans who become gods, humans descended from gods, and even lesser gods turned into humans as a judgment by superior gods. But here is Supreme God voluntarily becoming a man!

What kind of person would He be? He would be wonderful—

awe-inspiring, the ultimate. He would be not only *a* counselor, but *the* Counselor, the wisest, the One with whom wisdom begins and ends. Omniscient, all-knowing, one of the characteristics that are definitive of deity. But His wisdom is not theoretical; it is practical and relevant—wisdom that is directed toward us, available for our benefit. He would be the most caring, the most concerned.

Yet He is the mighty God, the warrior God, all-powerful. (Omnipotence is another of the divine attributes.) He is strong enough to withstand Tiglath-pileser—powerful enough to push him back, to annihilate him and all the powers that would raise their ugly heads against God's chosen.

"The Everlasting Father." Do we have some mixed communications here? Is Isaiah speaking of the first person of the Godhead or the second? Remember that there is no inherent ranking in deity. "First Person," "Second Person," and "Third Person" are terms we apply as a matter of communicative convenience; they are not terms God uses. The three Persons are one—in power, in purpose, in prerogatives. It was only to attain our salvation that an apparent hierarchy was established—by decree, according to Psalm 2:7, not by essence. (See Isaiah 63:16 and 64:8 for further identification of Yahweh, the second person of the Godhead, as divine Father.)

The Second Person is our Father by virtue of His having created us. "For by Him [Jesus] all things were created that are in heaven and that are on earth, visible and invisible. . . . All things were created through Him and for Him. And He is before all things, and in Him all things consist" (Col. 1:16, 17). Isaiah would have agreed with that last sentence, that Jesus exists from eternity to eternity—"everlasting," he called Him.

"Everlasting Father." Again there is that connotation of loving care, of protection, of interest in our eternal welfare. What a warm feeling Isaiah's description provides!

But there is more. "Prince of Peace." How nice the words sound slipping off the tongue. No doubt Isaiah's original words sounded as welcome to the ears of his Hebrew listeners. We all want peace. We do not need a Tiglath-pileser hammering at our gates in order to appreciate calm and quiet, security and freedom.

But peace is founded upon righteousness. That is as true in the political world as in the realm of the spirit. A nation at peace is one in which governor and governed are in harmony with each other, as well as in harmony with their neighbors. They all do right by each other. Isaiah understood that. "The work of righteousness will be peace," he said, "and the effect of righteousness, quietness and assurance forever" (Isa. 32:17).

That is what the Messiah would bring. Not only would He be the one who reigns in peace; He is the Prince, the Author, the Source of peace. "The government will be upon His shoulder"—the government of peoples, of worlds, of universes. "Of the increase of His government and peace there will be no end" (Isa. 9:7).

Is Isaiah moving into a third plane of prophecy here? Could it be that he is making reference to the *second* coming of Jesus? "Upon the throne of David and over His kingdom, to order it and establish it with judgment and justice from that time forward, even forever" (verse 7).

Although Jesus proclaimed His kingdom when He was here on earth, He spoke of His spiritual kingdom. He did not then take the throne of David (much to the disappointment of His disciples). His kingdom of glory begins when rebellion has been cast down and all nations acclaim His right to rule.

Some of Isaiah's descriptions of the Messiah seem paradoxical. "There shall come forth a Rod from the stem of Jesse, and a Branch shall grow out of his roots" (Isa. 11:1). "He shall strike the earth with the rod of His mouth, and with the breath of His lips He shall slay the wicked" (verse 4). Yet, "with righteousness He shall judge the poor, and decide with equity for the meek of the earth" (verse 4).

Again, in chapter 42: "He will not cry out, nor raise His voice, nor cause His voice to be heard in the street. A bruised reed He will not break, and smoking flax He will not quench" (verses 2 and 3). But "He will bring forth justice for truth. He will not fail nor be discouraged" (verses 3 and 4).

Strength with patience; justice with kindness. That is what our God is like. He is strong against sin, but understanding and receptive with the repentant sinner.

More than any other Old Testament writer, Isaiah understood the universal scope of God's grace. While his countrymen became more and more insular and selfish with their religion, this prophet-statesman opened the door of hope to "the islands of the sea," the Gentiles. "For the Gentiles shall seek Him" (Isa. 11:10). "I, the Lord, have called You in righteousness, and will hold Your hand; I will keep You and give You as a covenant to the people, as a light to the Gentiles" (Isa. 42:6). "The people who walked in darkness have seen a great light; those who dwelt in the land of the shadow of death, upon them a light has shined" (Isa. 9:2).

The disciples of Jesus had occasion to review those words after His ascension. Peter had a dream of a sheet filled with unclean animals. Under inspiration of the Holy Spirit, he understood the dream to mean that God cared for the Gentile as well as for the Jew. As his companions pondered his story, they must have remembered and studied Isaiah's message. The grace of God, the gospel of Jesus Christ, did indeed embrace the whole world.

The prophecies of Isaiah encompass the Messiah's incarnation, His divinity, His paternal and caring nature, His power and glory. And he confirms the endlessness of His reign, from everlasting to forever. But best of all, these qualities of the Messiah are manifest for *our* benefit. It is for us that He exercises His great power and wisdom. It is our peace that He establishes; it is in our behalf that He rules in justice and righteousness. How did Peter put it? The prophets "prophesied of the grace that would come to you."

Lake Michigan can experience some terrible, life-threatening storms. In fact, people do lose their lives on that inland sea. During one storm a ship began to break apart just offshore. A strong young man braved the icy waters to bring in weary and beleaguered passengers from the vessel. Not once or twice, but 19 times he swam through the crashing breakers to rescue helpless souls.

Years later a lecturer told the story. He was interrupted by a cry that the young man sat in the audience. Immediately the lecturer called him up front for an on-the-spot interview. "What one thing about that experience has stood out in your mind?" he asked the hero.

Said the young man, "The one thing I cannot forget is that out of the entire 19, not one ever came to thank me."

Have you thanked your Saviour lately?

Details of
the Promise

3

We began the previous chapter with a "suppose" situation. Let's try another. This time I have asked you to meet my brother at the airport, and you have agreed. Of course, you will need to know on which day, which flight, and at what time he will arrive.

But this is Washington, D.C.'s Dulles International Airport. Hundreds of passengers arrive on each flight. You could do as many do—stand at the arrival gate and hold up a sign that says "Woolsey." My brother would see it as he deplanes, and would identify himself as the one you are looking for.

But in our situation an enemy is involved. Knowing our plans, he could easily impersonate my brother. So I describe him. He is 65 years old. He's tall, as I am, more than six feet, but a bit slimmer, perhaps 175 pounds. He has a mustache. He will be wearing a low-key, plaid jacket. And here's the kicker: He will be carrying a copy of the *Adventist Review*. (That last touch was one that church representatives once used to identify themselves when visiting overseas stations for the first time.)

As soon as Adam and Eve sinned, God announced that He had a plan to accomplish their restoration. But He could not disclose it all at once, not immediately. In part, this was because they could not assimilate it. But also, had God given all the details right away, it would have been easy for Satan to impersonate the Redeemer.

Just when God developed the plan is difficult to say. John the revelator says the Lamb (Jesus) was "slain from the foundation of the world" (Rev. 13:8). Jesus did not die until many centuries after the world was created, but that He *would* die was so definitely ordained that it could be spoken of as a fait accompli, an "accomplished fact."

Paul puts the timing back further. He says we were chosen in Christ our Redeemer *before* the foundation of the world (see Eph. 1:4). This is in harmony with Peter. Speaking of Christ as "a lamb without blemish and without spot," Peter says, "He indeed was foreordained before the foundation of the world" (1 Peter 1:19, 20).

Further, Paul says that the "mystery of Christ"—the ministry of grace whereby God would accomplish the redemption of sinners—"from the beginning of the ages has been hidden in God" (Eph. 3:4, 9).

We know from many scriptures that Adam and Adam's world were not God's first handiwork. As the premier creation on this earth, Adam was called a "son of God" (Luke 3:38). The book of Job indicates there are other "sons of God" (Job 1:6; 2:1). There would be, therefore, other inhabited worlds, each with its chieftain. These, along with the angels, would comprise the "principalities and powers in the heavenly places" (Eph. 3:10) to whom God eventually revealed the mystery Paul spoke of.

If we understand correctly Paul's expression "the beginning of the ages" (verse 9), it would indicate that when God first created these free and intelligent beings, He recognized the theoretical possibility that they might use their freedom to rebel against Him. It was then that the three persons of the Godhead met in a "counsel of peace" (Zech. 6:13). Together They worked out a contingency plan.

According to this plan, one member of the Godhead would subject Himself to another in a relationship analogous to son and father. The one would be the servant, rendering perfect obedience as a demonstration of the validity of God's law. He would sacrifice His life as a vicarious atonement for transgression. The other would officially receive the sacrifice and effect the reconciliation (cf. Ps. 2:7; Acts 13:33; and Phil. 2:5-8).

The Holy Spirit would serve as the active, dynamic agent throughout the process. He would bring to bear God's power both in the life of the Son as He subjected Himself to the Father and in the sinner as he or she responded to the divine initiative.

Upon Adam's transgression, when he effectively sold himself

and his generations into Satan's hands, the loyal angels of heaven and the inhabitants of the other worlds were dismayed and confused. When God revealed to them the plan that had already been prepared, they were even more confounded.

They could not understand how God could give up His life—the very life that sustained them; but even less could they understand why. They offered to make the sacrifice themselves. But God explained that only the Author of life could give life. Only the Author of the law could atone for the transgression of the law. Besides, it was a demonstration of *His* love—which Satan had disparaged—love not only for Adam and Eve but for all the rest of His creation too.

With that explanation, "the morning stars sang together, and all the sons of God shouted for joy" (Job 38:7).

God revealed His plan to Adam and Eve as well, the ones who needed the plan. Even before He told them of the hardships they would bear—the curse on the earth, the pain of childbirth, the pangs of death—God held out the promise of redemption from the consequences of the terrible choice(s) they had made. "I will put enmity between you [the serpent, or Satan] and the woman, and between your seed and her Seed; He shall bruise your head, and you shall bruise His heel" (Gen. 3:15).

Notice that in these succinct words, even as God promised triumph over Satan and his dominion, He indicated that that triumph would come through one born into the human race—through "her Seed." Further, that victory would be at a divine price—the Seed would have His heel bruised.

After putting the sinful pair out of the Garden of Eden, God elaborated His plan. And He instituted the system of animal sacrifices, whereby mankind would remember both the promise and the divine price that would be paid in keeping it. The wages of sin is death, either the death of the sinner or the death of One who vicariously accepts the sinner's guilt. Adam and Eve rejoiced in the hope that the plan held forth, even as they grieved that their choice had brought matters to such a pass.

But the plan could not be implemented immediately. Satan had misrepresented God before the entire universe. The stakes were cosmic in scale. God had to win the allegiance of the universe by the demonstration of His premises as contrasted to Satan's allegations. And that would take time.

So here on earth the days multiplied into years, and the years into ages. Satan knew of God's plan, and he did everything he could to circumvent or nullify it. In the hearts of mankind the promise dimmed, the hope faded. Men and women steeped themselves in the worship of creatures instead of the Creator.

God called Abram from among the idolaters of Mesopotamia to the plains of Canaan. There were idolaters there too, but separated from his relatives in Ur, Abram could establish a distinct people who would provide an honest witness of the true God—and through whom God could fulfill His promise. "In your seed all the nations of the earth shall be blessed," God told Abraham (Gen. 22:18), in reference to the Redeemer.

This same promise was made to Isaac, Abraham's heir (Gen. 26:4), and to Jacob, Isaac's son (Gen. 28:14). From that time God often referred to the promise of the Redeemer in terms of the "covenant" He had made with Abraham, Isaac, and Jacob (Ex. 3:15, 16; Lev. 26:42; 2 Kings 13:23; Ps. 105:9, 10). Even in the New Testament, to be a child of Abraham was understood to mean being an heir of the promise of salvation (Matt. 8:11; Acts 3:25; Gal. 3:29).

As the years went by, more and more details were added to the promise. On his deathbed in Egypt, Jacob called his 12 sons to his side. After the custom of his time, to each he gave a blessing or a curse, and sometimes both. His words to Judah, his fourth son, are significant: "The scepter shall not depart from Judah, nor a lawgiver from between his feet, until Shiloh comes; and to Him shall be the obedience of the people" (Gen. 49:10).

Although the exact significance of the word "Shiloh" has been disputed, "most commentators, both Jewish and Christian, agree in regarding this as a Messianic prophecy" (Robert Jamieson et al., *A Commentary on the Old and New Testaments,* vol. 1, p. 267). The most commonly held meaning of the term is "man of peace," or "peace keeper." Ellen G. White supports the meaning of the term as "peace giver" *(The Desire of Ages,* p. 52). Thus Jacob revealed through which tribe of his 12 sons the Redeemer would be born.

Moreover, the last clause quoted from Jacob indicates, through a plural Hebrew word, that more than just the descendants of Jacob (Israel) would gather to the Messiah. This would be the fulfillment of the promise to Abraham that "all the nations of the earth" would be blessed by the Coming One.

A few hundred years later we find the children of Israel on their way out of Egypt, bound for the land promised to Abraham. On the way they contended with many problems—enemy tribes, serpents, internal rebellions, even an extremely serious reversal at the very threshold of their goal. The nationhood of Israel, the covenant made with Abraham, the promise of a Redeemer, seemed in jeopardy.

One of these threats appeared in the form of the Moabite and Midianite nations. Poised to throw their armies into battle against the Israelites, the two kings first tried an alternative. They engaged the services of the prophet Balaam to curse the intruders. But instead of a curse, Balaam gave the people of the promise just the encouraging word they needed at that time.

Balaam had a vision, he declared, in which he saw "the Almighty" and so had "the knowledge of the Most High" (Num. 24:16). He continued: "I see Him, but not now; I behold Him, but not near; a Star shall come out of Jacob; a Scepter shall rise out of Israel" (verse 17). More than a thousand years later the Magi of the East would be studying that prophecy.

Just before his death Moses made a significant contribution to the growing body of evidence regarding the coming Prince. He quoted the Lord: "I will raise up for them a Prophet like you [Moses] from among their brethren, and will put My words in His mouth, and He shall speak to them all that I command Him" (Deut. 18:18).

To David was given an especially portentous promise. At a point in his reign when his people were prospering, David proposed to build a temple to the Lord that would replace the tabernacle of animal skins which had served for so many years. The Lord was pleased with David's intentions, but through the prophet Nathan indicated He had other plans in that regard. Nevertheless, He assured David that his lineage on the throne would continue forever.

Note the words: "I will set up your seed after you, who will come from your body, and I will establish his kingdom" (2 Sam.

7:12). On the face of it, this would seem to refer to David's immediate successor, and that was the primary application. But David,
through the inspiration of the Holy Spirit, found in the words more
than that. With quickening pulse he realized God had just
promised that the world's Messiah would come through his
progeny (Acts 2:30). Overwhelmed with the wonderful revelation,
David could only sit speechless before the Lord in the tabernacle.

As more time passed, prophecies of the Messiah came relatively thick and fast. John L. Shuler, a successful Seventh-day
Adventist evangelist of an earlier time, used to give a sermon enti-
tled "The Man Who Wrote His Own Autobiography Before He
Was Born." His point was that Jesus, the Yahweh (Lord) of the
Old Testament, directed the prophets in giving many and various
details of the life He would live when He entered the human race.

First there was delineated, as we have seen, that He would
come through Abraham's children; that was narrowed to the tribe
of Judah, then to the royal lineage of David.

Isaiah described His virgin birth (Isa. 7:14). Micah pinpointed
the very village in which He would be born (Micah 5:2). Jeremiah
foresaw the massacre of the innocents, fulfilled when Herod tried
to destroy a possible threat to his own throne (Jer. 31:15). And
Hosea found Him fleeing to Egypt for refuge (Hosea 11:1).

Some prophecies portrayed the nature of the Messiah's public
ministry, such as the power of His discourses, likened to Elijah
(Mal. 4:5, 6) and His use of parables (Ps. 78:2, 3).

The larger number of the prophecies about Jesus center around
the closing scenes of His life. There was His triumphal entry into
Jerusalem (Zech. 9:9), His betrayal by a close friend (Ps. 41:9), the
brutality demonstrated against Him at His trial (Zech. 13:7), and
the fact that His conviction would be obtained at the hand of false
witnesses (Ps. 27:12).

The 30 pieces of silver that fell from Judas' hand were seen in
prophetic vision hundreds of years earlier (Zech. 11:12, 13), as
were the soldiers casting lots for His outer cloak (Ps. 22:18). That
He would be vilely mistreated (Isa. 50:6), yet would not rail against
His tormenters (Ps. 109:4) was included in the Divine Record.

The condemned Messiah would be given vinegar to drink (Ps.
69:21); He would be pierced (Zech. 12:10), executed as a common

criminal (Isa. 53:12), yet no bones would be broken (Ps. 34:20). He would be buried in a rich man's grave (Isa. 53:9).

But through all this there was the glad message that the Redeemer would not be held captive in the grave. "You will not leave my soul in Sheol," writes David under inspiration, "nor will You allow Your Holy One to see corruption" (Ps. 16:10). And following His resurrection, the Son of David would be restored to His rightful place on the throne of heaven (Ps. 110:1).

Now, if you have been looking up all these references, you may have noticed one outstanding fact—many of them would not appear to a newcomer to the Word of God as referring to the world's Redeemer. It may seem that we have been reading back into long-ago statements meanings that were not intended when they were written.

We might be open to such a charge were it not that inspiration has already made the connections for us. The Gospel of Matthew is replete with such references. It seems Matthew took delight in looking up as many fulfilled prophecies as he could find. Some say that is the main purpose of his Gospel. To Jesus' disciples, when they were so disheartened over His death, He effectively used these prophecies to show them that His death was part of the divine plan. They hadn't thought of that.

But if God intended that these references be understood as applying to the Messiah, why wasn't the point made more clearly? And why didn't He come out with all of it, all at once? We may not understand all God's reasons, but some good ones come to mind.

Satan could have taken advantage of the open details and more easily deceived God's people. As it was, he led many to proclaim themselves as the fulfillment of the people's hope. False messiahs appeared on the scene before Christ as well as after Him.

Also, the very procedure of digging out the meaning of the prophecies was a faith-building exercise for students of the Word. Just as physical exercise builds bodies, so study and prayer and a personal relationship with God builds character.

Then we note Jesus' words to His disciples regarding His departure: "Now I have told you before it comes, that when it does come to pass, you may believe" (John 14:29). Some things we are not supposed to know ahead of time. Our faith is built by holding on to God without knowing just how He will bring about His promises. (This passage may have a bearing on prophecies of the last days as well. Perhaps we run ahead of God when we try to chart just what all the details of Revelation mean and how all the end-time events will fit together.)

Peter used these prophecies in his Jerusalem sermon (Acts 2). As for Paul, every time he came to a new town he would first head for the synagogue and show the Jews there, by means of these prophecies, that their long-awaited Messiah had come (Acts 13:13-43). We may be thankful that God has preserved these prophecies for our edification as well so that through the study of the Scriptures we may believe on Jesus Christ and be saved.

The Appointed Time

4

Years ago Edwin A. Abbott in the book *Flatland* imagined a place and race where there were only two dimensions, length and breadth. The only way the inhabitants of this land could envision their world was edge-on—thus, everything blended into one long, extremely thin line. As he developed this bit of fantasy, the creatures could not "see" at all, for there was nothing to see; they could only feel their way around—yes, they had some mobility. And so they learned to recognize each other and their environs by touch, by the number and acuity of corners and angles, by the arc of curves.

In contrast to that never-never land, we enjoy a world of three dimensions, for we deal also with height. We are usually rather comfortable in our concepts of these three—we can manipulate them to our liking. If we have a board that is too long, we cut it off. If we have something that is too short, we can add to it or perhaps stretch it.

These three dimensions define space for us. But there are some aspects of space that disturb us, for we do not understand them. We can measure the distance to the sun and moon; we can even calculate the span to the farthest galaxy detectable by technology. But when we realize there may be more beyond that, our mind boggles. We cannot fathom a universe that goes on and on, without boundaries, without an end.

But there is a fourth dimension, that of time. This also disturbs us, because although we can measure time, we cannot manipulate

31

it. We can neither shorten nor stretch it. We cannot start or stop it. Rather, time rules us, and not only in the hectic pace of our days. We are born without our choosing, and we die whether we are ready or not. We are all familiar with the tyranny of time.

But God is the master of time. He created time, just as He created space. He can start time or stop it. He can stretch it out, as He did for Joshua in the battle with the Amorites. He can turn time back, as He did for Hezekiah. "With the Lord one day is as a thousand years, and a thousand years as one day" (2 Peter 3:8). Not only does God control time, but also He can read history before it happens. He knows the end from the beginning. "New things I declare; before they spring forth I tell you of them" (Isa. 42:9).

But although God is not bound by time, He knows that we are, and so He takes time into account in His dealings with human beings. To the men and women of the antediluvian race He announced that they had but 120 more years. Noah took advantage of the extension by building an ark wherein he and his family were delivered from the Flood. All the others squandered their allotment of time.

One night God appeared to Abraham to reassure him regarding the promise that he would be the father of a great nation. The future would not all be rosy, God pointed out. Included in the nation-building would be an extended period spent in servitude to a foreign power. "Your descendants will be strangers in a land that is not theirs, and will serve them, and they will afflict them four hundred years" (Gen. 15:13).

Why should God include affliction in a foreign land as an element in the future of this faithful patriarch's progeny? And why worry him by telling him about it? On the one hand, the experience would help the family cohere, to recognize their identity as a nation. Were they to remain in Canaan, likely they would intermarry with the Canaanites, scatter like the nomads of the area, and never know cohesiveness. On the other hand, the time limit would be a source of hope during their affliction. As the years passed, they could look for light at the end of the tunnel.

Jonah was another man given a time prophecy. He was sent to warn the people of Nineveh that within 40 days the city would be destroyed. But they experienced a reprieve. Unlike the people before the Flood, the Ninevites repented of their wickedness. God gladly accepted their contrition and spared the city.

To Jeremiah God gave a prophecy similar to the one He gave Abraham. The Jewish people would be captives again, this time in Babylon. They would languish there for 70 years (Jer. 25:11, 12).

Then to Daniel God gave the most stupendous time prophecy of all. This prophecy held all the elements of the previous ones— the warning to Noah's and Jonah's generations, the hope embodied in Abraham's and Jeremiah's messages. But best of all, this prophecy to Daniel announced the appearance of none other than the Messiah Himself.

For thousands of years the human race had groaned under Satan's heel, but it was buoyed by the promise of a Redeemer to be born of a woman. Pregnant mothers in every generation had wondered if their child might be the One. Hints and snippets of hope had been shared with Adam and Eve; they had come through Enoch, through Abraham and Moses. Balaam had referred to Him; David and Isaiah described Him. But when? When would the long night of satanic captivity end?

To God, time was not a compelling factor, but He knew that men and women are limited; they live in time. And so He provided through Daniel a beacon light to encourage and guide them.

As was his habit, Daniel was praying in his chambers one day, between official duties at the royal court. The immediate subject of his prayer was Jeremiah's 70-year prophecy. For nearly that long his people had suffered bondage, first under the Babylonians then under their successors, the Persians. Earlier, Daniel had received a vision that seemed to indicate God was about to act decisively in human affairs. Could it be the coming of the Messiah? But the vision also included a hint that there would be a considerable delay in its fulfillment.

Daniel prayed that God would honor His promise of deliverance. He was aware that, as Moses had warned 900 years earlier, if Israel didn't live up to their part of the covenant relationship with God, God was under no obligation to deliver on His part. So Daniel prayed, first a prayer of contrition and repentance on the part of his people. Then he prayed that God would come through and not hold them in captivity longer than the 70 years.

Now we see an example of God's supremacy over space and time. Before Daniel finished praying—and it was not a long prayer (it is recorded in 16 verses in Daniel 9)—no less than the archangel Gabriel, the one whose official position is by the side of God, appeared at Daniel's side. He had been commanded to "fly swiftly," we are told, in response to the prophet's appeal.

Gabriel got right to the point. "Seventy weeks are determined for your people and for your holy city," he said (Dan. 9:24).

The Hebrew word for "weeks" here is literally translated "sevens" (see NIV). It is most often used to mean a seven-day week. But in prophecies not everything is literal. Seventy literal weeks is less than a year and a half. That is not a realistic time period to apply to a prophecy involving the rebuilding of Jerusalem. It could take that long just to mount a caravan of people and materials to go there from Babylon! On the other hand, in Daniel 10:2, 3, the prophet wants to specify three seven-day weeks, so he uses a term that literally is translated "weeks of days."

So in Daniel 9:24 we are justified in assuming the angel spoke of weeks of years rather than days. Seventy weeks of years would be 490 years.

(Another time-honored method of interpreting this passage applies the day-for-a-year principle. Ezekiel, a prophet contemporary to Daniel, was told to lie on his right side for 40 days, each day representing one year of siege of Jerusalem. When Israel was about to enter Canaan from Egypt, they sent spies into the land. The spies spent 40 days checking things out, then returned with a negative report. The Israelites rebelled against God, saying they would rather have stayed in Egypt. In response, God told them they would spend 40 years in the wilderness, one year of wandering for each day the unfaithful spies had been in the Promised Land. Applying this method to Daniel 9:24, each day of the 70 years Gabriel spoke of meant one literal year.)

This period, 490 years, was to be allotted to Daniel's people, who, of course, were the Jews. His "holy city" was Jerusalem, which had fallen to Nebuchadnezzar when Daniel was a teenager.

Gabriel spoke on. This 490-year period would encompass a number of very important accomplishments: "to finish the transgression, to make an end of sins, to make reconciliation for iniquity, to bring in everlasting righteousness, to seal up vision and prophecy, and to anoint the Most Holy" (verse 24). That sounds like the climax to the great plan of salvation! If not the actual climax, at least the setting into motion that which would effectively lead to the climax. Think of it! Everlasting righteousness; an end to sin!

Gabriel began to explain: "Know therefore and understand, that from the going forth of the command to restore and build Jerusalem [ah, there we have a starting point for the 490 years] until Messiah the Prince, there shall be seven weeks and sixty-two weeks; the street shall be built again, and the wall, even in troublesome times" (verse 23).

Here was an actual schedule given for the appearance of the much-desired Messiah! I am sure Daniel was beside himself. He probably had a hard time concentrating on what else Gabriel had to say.

But the archangel had crucial details to add. "And after the sixty-two weeks Messiah shall be cut off, but not for Himself. . . . Then he shall confirm a covenant with many for one week; but in the middle of the week He shall bring an end to sacrifice and offering" (verses 26, 27).

Just as Daniel and his people had been removed in stages from Jerusalem, so their freedom to return came in increments. First was a simple permit from Cyrus, king of Persia, for the Jews to return to Jerusalem and rebuild the Temple. Darius I ordered the non-Jews in the surrounding area to stop their harassment of the project. The final and empowering decree came from Artaxerxes Longimanus. In 457 B.C. he gave official status to the Jews in their homeland, establishing their political autonomy and even providing financial means for the reconstruction.

From this point in time, Gabriel said, Daniel could count 69 weeks, or 483 years, to the Messiah the Prince. That brings us to A.D. 27. What happened in that year? Extrapolating from Luke's Gospel (chapter 3), that is when Jesus was baptized and anointed with the Holy Spirit to enter upon His official work. *Messiah,* a Hebrew word, means "anointed one." So does *christos,* or Christ, in Greek.

Gabriel said the Messiah would continue to honor His covenant with the Jewish people for one week, or seven more years. In the middle of that week He would bring an end to sin. Three and a half years after His anointing as the Messiah, Jesus gave His life on the cross, providing an atonement for the world's transgressions.

But all this was future to Daniel. Probably he did not see the details as clearly as we can in hindsight. But what was important to him and his people was that an actual time had been set for the appearance of the Messiah. In the years that followed, the Jews pored over this prophecy. It provided hope during the dark years of oppression by Antiochus Epiphanes, the Herods, and Roman emperors. And not only the Jews anticipated the Messiah. Remember the Magi? They had more than a star to stir their hearts—they, too, were students of the prophecy.

Meanwhile, Persian rule gave way to Greek dominance. Greek culture, especially the language, spread throughout the so-called civilized world. It became the lingua franca, the common tongue that provided communication for peoples far removed from each other.

More so than in trade, Greek was the language of literature. Rich in vocabulary, replete with nuances and inflections, the Greek language was most suitable for expressing ethics, feelings, and emotions, and the abstract concepts of religious thought. Even the Romans, who conquered the Greeks in warfare and politics, were debtors to the Greeks in matters of culture and art.

But the Romans made significant contributions in other ways. With their strength of arms they were able to subjugate a much larger area of the earth. From Celtic Britain to the Caspian Sea and the Persian Gulf, from the Teutonic tribes in northern Europe to deep into the African continent, the Roman fasces, emblem of authority, held sway. Not only did this Roman presence enforce political stability, it also meant free and easy travel and commerce between provinces that, as erstwhile nations, had been in constant conflict. The *Pax Romana,* or Roman peace, was a major fact of life.

Besides building a political empire, the Romans were great builders of infrastructure—aqueducts, coliseums, and, what is more important to this study, they built great roads and bridges. These were initially for the use of the army, to be able to get to far-flung reaches of the empire quickly. But they were used by the common people as well, contributing to the fluidity and flow of thoughts and ideas, as well as of commerce.

This was the time for the Messiah to appear: a common language, widely used and of high literary quality; universal peace and political stability; ease of travel and transportation. And there were Jews everywhere.

Initially scattered in the Diaspora, the forced resettlement of Jews by Assyrians and Babylonians, only some had returned to Jerusalem under the grants of Cyrus, Darius, and Artaxerxes. Many more elected to stay where they had put down roots. These Jews were candidates to receive the gospel of the Messiah as they came periodically to Jerusalem for religious festivals. Then they could be catalysts of divine grace to their neighbors in their adopted homelands.

"When the fullness of the time had come, God sent forth His Son, born of a woman, born under the law, to redeem those who were under the law, that we might receive the adoption of sons" (Gal. 4:4, 5). So God had a timetable, and when the time came, He acted.

But was God limited by time? Did He have to wait for everything on earth to be ready before Jesus came? Probably not. Remember that the conflict between Satan and God began in heaven. Its first casualties were angels. From the start, that warfare has had cosmic ramifications.

Sometimes in our egocentricity we forget that God has intelligent creatures on other worlds. They too have the power of choice. Had God destroyed Satan too soon, before these beings could be satisfied in their own minds that he deserved to be done away with, they would have either served God from fear of similar catastrophe or rebelled against His "autocratic" heavy-handedness.

Neither alternative was satisfactory with God. So He allowed Satan enough time and enough latitude to demonstrate his true nature, the moral bankruptcy of his claims, and the inherent inadequacy of his false system. When that point came, God sent forth His Son. He sent Him "that through death He might destroy him who had the power of death, that is, the devil" (Heb. 2:14). He sent Him "to finish the transgression, to make an end of sins, to make reconciliation for iniquity, to bring in everlasting righteousness" (Dan. 9:24).

Blessed be the name of the Lord!

The Mystery of Godliness

5

What happened?

We have noted how Jesus fulfilled the prophecies of the Old Testament that foretold the Messiah. They described the circumstances of His birth, how He would carry forth His public ministry, and many details centered around His arrest, death, and resurrection.

But many of those prophecies stressed the stature He would possess as Messiah. The very first one, to Adam and Eve, indicated He would be a conqueror. Balaam called Him a star and a scepter. He was promised to King David as a successor to his throne, and both Isaiah and Daniel saw Him as a Prince who would reestablish the people of the covenant with the prosperity David had enjoyed in his reign.

But that is not the way things turned out. Jesus was born in Bethlehem, as prophesied, but had only a manger for His bed! He grew up in Nazareth of Galilee, definitely the "other side of the tracks" as far as His contemporaries were concerned. He had no "real" education, and though He attracted a following, no one who counted on the national scene was included in His camp. Even though some tried to crown Him, He would not accept kingship. To top it all off, He was executed as a common criminal!

Well, we hadn't examined all the prophecies. There are others that foretold His suffering and humiliation. Some of these are by the same prophet who portrayed best His majesty and divinity!

With Isaiah 52:13 the prophet begins a section described as

pertaining to the "suffering Servant" and understood by most Christian commentators as referring to the Messiah. The passage continues through the fifty-third chapter—actually, there should not be a chapter break in the passage at all.

This chapter has been described as "the most central, the deepest, and the loftiest thing that the Old Testament prophecy, outstripping itself, has ever achieved" (Franz Delitzsch, *Biblical Commentaries on the Prophecies of Isaiah,* vol. 2, p. 303; quoted in M. L. Andreasen, *Isaiah, the Gospel Prophet,* vol. 2, p. 86).

Isaiah speaks of the Messiah as "despised and rejected by men, a man of sorrows and acquainted with grief" (verse 3). "He was oppressed and He was afflicted, yet He opened not His mouth" (verse 7). But this maltreatment was not for anything He had done: "Surely He has borne our griefs and carried our sorrows" (verse 4), yet "He had done no violence, nor was any deceit in His mouth" (verse 9).

Especially note the fifth verse: "He was wounded for our transgressions, He was bruised for our iniquities; the chastisement of our peace was upon Him, and by His stripes we are healed." This verse is the Old Testament equivalent, if you will, of John 3:16.

Most Jewish—and even some Christian—commentators do not recognize this passage as referring to the Messiah. They cling to the concept of a Prince, a King, a Conqueror. Yet from the very first time humanity sinned and God promised redemption, it was clear that restoration would be at the price of the Redeemer's life.

Adam and Eve were under the curse of death because of their sin. If they did not die, it would be only because Someone died in their stead. To remind them of that fact, God instructed Adam and Eve to initiate the system of animal sacrifices. The suffering Messiah is inherent in the sacrificial system, so central to ancient Hebrew worship.

When God promised Abram (Abraham) that, though he was presently childless, his seed would inherit the land the patriarch was camping on, Abram asked, "How shall I know that I will inherit it?" God told Abram to take a heifer, a goat, a ram, a turtledove, and a pigeon. Each animal, except the birds, was cut into two pieces, and piled in two heaps. That night in vision God appeared to Abram. He passed between the two piles of sacrifice and repeated His promise.

Interestingly, this type of covenant is still practiced among no-
madic peoples in the Middle East. It signifies that the covenant
makers pledge their lives. If they do not keep the covenant, they
are to be cut up like the animal. So God was pledging His very existence in covenant with Abraham. Referring to this occasion,
Jesus said that "Abraham rejoiced to see My day, and he saw it
and was glad" (John 8:56).

We note that these specific animals and birds that Abraham
sacrificed were the very same as those used by the children of
Israel in their more elaborate sacrificial system. Every time they
offered a sacrifice in the wilderness tabernacle or later in the
Temple, they were perpetuating the covenant God had made with
their father Abraham.

According to the system established by Moses when the tabernacle was built, when a person sinned he was to bring an animal to
the gate of the tabernacle, lay his hands on its head in confession
of his sins, and kill the animal. Its blood would be carried and
sprinkled inside the tabernacle (Lev. 4:1-6). Once a year an animal
would be sacrificed in behalf of all the people. "For the life of the
flesh is in the blood," God said, "and I have given it to you upon
the altar to make atonement for your souls; for it is the blood that
makes atonement for the soul" (Lev. 17:11).

Yet it is not blood that God wants. He is not a sadistic, blood-
thirsty demon. "Will I eat the flesh of bulls, or drink the blood of
goats?" He asks (Ps. 50:13). " 'To what purpose is the multitude of
your sacrifices to Me?' says the Lord. . . . 'I do not delight in the
blood of bulls, or of lambs or goats' " (Isa. 1:11). Instead, "Cease
to do evil, learn to do good" (verses 16, 17).

" 'Come now, and let us reason together,' says the Lord,
'Though your sins are like scarlet, they shall be as white as snow;
though they are red like crimson, they shall be as wool' " (verse 18).

Isaiah points out that the Messiah is the antitype of those animal sacrifices. He is the One given to the world as the covenant in
fulfillment of the promise made to Abraham: "I, the Lord, have
called You in righteousness, and will hold Your hand; I will keep
You and give You as a covenant to the people, as a light to the
Gentiles, to open blind eyes, to bring out prisoners from the prison,

those who sit in darkness from the prison house" (Isa. 42:6, 7).

The first covenant was made between God and humanity. Inasmuch as Jesus is both God and man, the covenant is complete in Him. He *is* the covenant.

The Messiah is the real Lamb whose blood atones for our sins. "The Lord has laid on Him the iniquity of us all. . . . He was led as a lamb to the slaughter. . . . He was cut off from the land of the living; for the transgressions of My people He was stricken" (Isa. 53:6-8).

Jesus alone could accomplish our salvation. Only the God-Man could reconcile fallen humans with immortal God. Only One who had life within Himself could give it to those who had forfeited the right to live.

But we have to acknowledge our sinfulness. We have to recognize our need for a Lamb. Again, this has been a problem from the start. When God first confronted our first father with his transgression, Adam tried to pin the blame on others—on the serpent, or on Eve, or even on God, who had given him his companion. The Pharisee in Jesus' parable thanked God that he was not like the publican—but he left unjustified, unforgiven.

We cannot help ourselves. Our hearts are "deceitful above all things, and desperately wicked" (Jer. 17:9). We can rid ourselves of sin no easier than we can change the color of our skin. We are like half-dead foundlings, thrown out into the field without having been washed, even without our navel cords cut (Eze. 16:4, 5).

Blind to our defects, we think we are something great—and want to be greater. As the brightest and highest angel in heaven, Lucifer was dissatisfied. His heart was lifted up because of his beauty; he corrupted his wisdom for the sake of his splendor (Eze. 28:17). He told himself, "I will ascend into heaven, I will exalt my throne above the stars of God. . . . I will be like the Most High" (Isa. 14:13, 14).

Then, cast out to this earth as Satan, he shared the same attitude with Eve. "God knows that in the day you eat of it [the forbidden fruit] your eyes will be opened and you will be like God" (Gen. 3:5). Eve liked that idea, and took the fruit and ate it. We have been trying to exalt ourselves ever since.

Satan even tried this same scheme on Jesus in the wilderness

(Matt. 4:3-12). He offered Jesus the kingdoms of the world, without pain or sacrifice. Wouldn't that be nice? King of all He surveyed! Satan took Jesus to the pinnacle of the Temple. "Jump off," he encouraged. "God will save you." In effect, this was saying that Jesus could tell God what to do, that by jumping He could bind God to perform in Jesus' behalf.

How can any creature exalt self to equal or surpass the Creator? That is indeed a conundrum. Paul calls it the "mystery of lawlessness." He speaks of the day when "the man of sin is revealed, the son of perdition, who opposes and exalts himself above all that is called God or that is worshiped, so that he sits as God in the temple of God, showing himself that he is God" (2 Thess. 2:3, 4). "For the mystery of lawlessness is already at work," Paul continues (verse 7).

We have a tendency to see God through the adversary's eyes: We know that He is "high and lifted up" (Isa. 6:1), surrounded with majesty and glory, the object of adoration by thousands of thousands of angels. *How great it would be to receive that kind of treatment,* we think. But we forget that God is also love. He is constantly working in behalf of His creatures, giving life, serving, caring.

It is human nature—the nature of fallen Adam—to take. He took the fruit that was not his. Cain took his brother's life. We say, "What's yours is mine, and I will keep it." But it is the divine nature to give. God says, "What's Mine is yours, and I will give it."

Of Christ we read, " 'I seek not mine own glory,' but the glory of Him that sent Me" (John 8:50). In these words is set forth the great principle which is the law of life for the universe. All things Christ received from God, but He took to give. So in the heavenly courts, in His ministry for all created beings: through the beloved Son, the Father's life flows out to all; through the Son it returns, in praise and joyous service, a tide of love, to the great Source of all. And thus through Christ the circuit of beneficence is complete, representing the character of the great Giver, the law of life" *(The Desire of Ages,* p. 21).

Jesus demonstrated this when He washed His disciples' feet. "Whoever desires to become great among you, let him be your servant. And whoever desires to be first among you, let him be your slave—just as the Son of Man did not come to be served, but to serve, and to give His life a ransom for many" (Matt. 20:26-28).

This is what Paul called the "mystery of godliness," in direct contrast to the mystery of lawlessness or iniquity. "Without controversy great is the mystery of godliness: God was manifested in the flesh, justified in the Spirit, seen by angels, preached among the Gentiles, believed on in the world, received up in glory" (1 Tim. 3:16).

The mystery of iniquity is exaltation of self. At its ultimate, this is seen in someone trying to take God's place, the creature impersonating the Creator. The mystery of godliness is the humbling of self. It is epitomized in Jesus coming to earth, taking human nature, living a humble life, dying a most ignominious death. In short, the Creator taking the place of His creatures.

Paul elaborates on this marvel: "The mystery which has been hidden from ages and from generations, but now has been revealed to His saints. To them God willed to make known what are the riches of the glory of this mystery among the Gentiles, which is Christ in you, the hope of glory" (Col. 1:26, 27). That is part of the mystery, not only that God would become a man, but that He would take up His dwelling within the human heart. He would so closely identify Himself with us that He seeks *to live in us.*

"For you know the grace of our Lord Jesus Christ, that though He was rich, yet for your sakes He became poor, that you through His poverty might become rich" (2 Cor. 8:9).

Sometimes we try to measure our spirituality by the things we "had to give up" in becoming a Christian. "I gave up smoking." "I gave up coffee." "I gave up all my rock music records. I had some good ones too." Sometimes we may even sound like we are not sure if we made a good bargain. I remember a church deacon hankering after the pork he had given up some 20 years earlier to become a Seventh-day Adventist. (Have you noticed that God never asks us to give up anything that's really good for us?)

But none of our sacrifices can compare with what Jesus gave up. From His position as ruler of the universe, He became a man on this small planet. He was born to a poor family, lived in a disreputable town in an insignificant province of a non-nation. He accepted emotional debasement, physical torture, and excruciating death as a criminal. More than this, He suffered exclusion from the presence and even the approbation of His Father, with whom He had been one since time immemorial.

The adjective "poor" is not enough to describe the depths of Jesus' sacrifice. He was poor in possessions, poor in the number of friends who would stand with Him, poor in terms of what this world calls accomplishments.

"Who is this who comes from Edom, with dyed garments from Bozrah, this One who is glorious in His apparel, traveling in the greatness of His strength?

" 'I who speak in righteousness, mighty to save.'

"Why is Your apparel red, and Your garments like one who treads in the winepress?

" 'I have trodden the winepress alone, and from the peoples no one was with Me' " (Isa. 63:1-3).

But "rich" does not adequately describe the gains we receive in direct consequence of Jesus' self-abnegation. No longer outcasts, half-dead foundlings, we are become sons and daughters of God. We are the lawful heirs of the King of kings and Lord of lords.

It is God's purpose for us that, having experienced in Christ the mystery of godliness, we should share in the same spirit. It is our privilege to share the mystery. "Through the knowledge of Him who called us by glory and virtue, by which have been given to us exceedingly great and precious promises, that through these you may be partakers of the divine nature, having escaped the corruption that is in the world through lust" (2 Peter 1:3, 4).

When Paul contemplated the great sacrifice of Jesus, he said, "I bow my knees to the Father of our Lord Jesus Christ, from whom the whole family in heaven and earth is named, that He would grant you, according to the riches of His glory, to be strengthened with might through His Spirit in the inner man, that Christ may dwell in your hearts through faith; that you, being rooted and grounded in love, may be able to comprehend with all the saints what is the width and length and depth and height—to know the love of Christ which passes knowledge; that you may be filled with all the fullness of God" (Eph. 3:14-19).

What is your response to Paul's prayer—to the sacrifice Jesus made in your stead? There comes to mind the words of a hymn:

THE MYSTERY OF GODLINESS

"Jesus, I my cross have taken,
All to leave and follow Thee;
All things else I have forsaken;
Thou from hence my all shalt be.
Perish every fond ambition,
All I've sought, or hoped, or known;
Yet how rich is my condition,
While I prove the Lord my own."
—Henry F. Lyte

Active
Love

6

Men and women hurry along the narrow village streets to the synagogue. In reality, that is their usual pace when they are on their way to worship. (In leaving, they are accustomed to walking slowly, reluctantly.) But on this Sabbath they have extra reason for haste. Rumor has it that Jesus will give the sermon this morning.

They know Jesus well—He grew up among them. A good man, like His mother and siblings. Hard workers, pious, quiet. But He left town a year and a half ago, just when His trade skills were receiving wide acclaim. Since then, they have been hearing great things about Him from down south—how He has healed the sick and the blind, even caused quite a commotion in the Temple once. Today they get to see Him—maybe He'll do a miracle just for them. It's a nice feeling to have a local boy make good in the world "outside."

In the synagogue the men sit in the main chamber, the women in a gallery to the rear. In an alcove in the front is the "ark" containing the scrolls of the Law and the Prophets. Steps lead up to this alcove, but a curtain hides it from view. In front of the ark is a row of seats facing the congregation. Seated here are the rulers of the synagogue and other dignitaries.

In the center of the synagogue is another elevated spot, surmounted by a desk or lectern and a chair.

Most of the seats are taken now. One of the last to enter is Jesus. A low murmur fills the room; the chief of the synagogue whispers to Jesus. Yes! He will speak.

But first there are other rituals; the whole service will take some time. Worship begins with two prayers and the recitation of the Shema, or statement of faith. There are several more prayers, some ritualistic, others of a more relevant nature. Eulogies and a benediction close this liturgical part of the service.

Then the attendant or deacon approaches the ark and takes down the Law—the Pentateuch, or five books of Moses. Hidden by the curtain, he carefully removes the scroll, rolled around two rods, from its case and cloth wrappings. He takes the Law to the lectern, where seven people take turns reading it, several verses each. The Law is written in Hebrew. Because most of the people present do not understand the original language of the Scriptures, an interpreter gives the Aramaic equivalent, verse by verse.

After returning the Law to its niche, the minister takes down the Prophets, scrolled around one rod. He opens it to the prophecy of Isaiah—probably at Jesus' request—and lays it on the lectern.

The congregation waits in hushed expectancy. Jesus mounts the steps and stands at the lectern. They have heard Him before in this synagogue, in the years when He was growing up. But this time is different. He is different, and not just in His weathered appearance.

"As the people looked upon Him, they saw a face where divine compassion was blended with conscious power. Every glance of the eye, every feature of the countenance, was marked with humility, and expressive of unutterable love. He seemed to be surrounded by an atmosphere of spiritual influence. While His manners were gentle and unassuming, He impressed men with a sense of power that was hidden, yet could not be wholly concealed. Was this the One for whom Israel had so long waited?" (*The Desire of Ages*, pp. 137, 138).

In a clear and carefully modulated voice Jesus begins to read the familiar words of Isaiah 61. The words are familiar because it is a favorite passage with these people. This is a promise of the coming of the Messiah, and every synagogue service includes some reference to that long-looked-for event. A special thrill stirs their hearts.

"The Spirit of the Lord is upon Me, because He has anointed Me to preach the gospel to the poor. He has sent Me to heal the brokenhearted, to preach deliverance to the captives and recovery of sight to the blind, to set at liberty those who are oppressed, to preach the acceptable year of the Lord" (Luke 4:18, 19).

Not exactly the same wording as Isaiah had it. It is not unusual for readers of the Prophets in the synagogue service to rearrange phrases, perhaps omit some. (Besides, in writing the account, Luke used the Greek Septuagint version rather than the Hebrew.)

After reading at the lectern, Jesus sits down to teach. All eyes are on Him, every ear straining to catch His first words: "Today this Scripture is fulfilled in your hearing" (verse 21). It is true! He is claiming the prophecy by applying it to Himself! Again there is that thrill of expectancy, the feeling that they are witnessing something very special. "There was a general stir of admiration; they were surprised that words of such grace should fall from his lips" (Luke 4:22, NEB). Hearts are moved by the Holy Spirit, and fervent "amens" filled the room.

"The Spirit of the Lord God is upon Me." Isaiah had earlier identified the Spirit in these words: "The Spirit of the Lord shall rest upon Him, the Spirit of wisdom and understanding, the Spirit of counsel and might, the Spirit of knowledge and of the fear of the Lord" (Isa. 11:2). Not seven Spirits, but seven characteristics of the Holy Spirit.

It was at His baptism that the Holy Spirit rested on Jesus officially. It was by this anointing that Jesus became the Messiah (Acts 10:38), which in Hebrew means "anointed"; the same with the Greek *christos,* or Christ.

In the Jewish system, three offices were bestowed by anointing—prophet, priest, and king (see 1 Chron. 29:22). Jesus was anointed as all three: He is prophet in that He preaches—He speaks to us for God; He is God's mouthpiece. Jesus is priest in that He heads up our worship in God—He represents us before the Father; He pleads our case. And Jesus is king in that He rules over all. Furthermore, He makes official proclamations: they become official because He makes them.

These three offices are included in the passage that Jesus read in the synagogue at Nazareth.

"The Spirit . . . has anointed Me to preach good tidings to the poor" (Isa. 61:1). The good tidings, of course, is the gospel itself, the good news of salvation, the news that God loves us. "Gospel" means good news; Mark points out that is how Jesus opened His ministry in Galilee, "preaching the gospel of the kingdom" (Mark 1:14).

That was one of Jesus' purposes in coming to earth, to tell people about God's goodness. Satan had distorted God's character. From the Garden of Eden, he had misled people about what God is like. Jesus came not only to tell them but to demonstrate God's goodness.

Jesus could speak, of course, from personal experience. Not only had He known the Father from eternity, but also in His earthly sojourn He saw constant reminders of the Father's love. "Jesus saw God everywhere. He walked at home in a universe which a heavenly Father had fashioned for His children" (Harvie Branscomb, *The Teachings of Jesus,* p. 148). Jesus drew lessons from this universe for His listeners—the lilies of the field, the sparrows, the sun and rain.

God's love is active. It reaches out and does things for His creatures—and continues to do them. "In some religions the divine being has been portrayed as content and satisfied, engaged only in self-contemplation. [There are some] pieces of religious literature which develop the thought that God is absolutely passive. He wants nothing. He needs nothing. His activity is concerned only with that which is perfect. *Jesus said that God cares" (ibid.,* pp. 154, 155).

Jesus came in behalf of the poor, not only to the poor in goods but especially to the "poor in spirit," that is, the humble, the teachable. Where would have been the hope of the lowly in life—and there are a lot more of them—had Jesus come as a king among us?

The fulfillment of this phrase is illustrated by—but not limited to—the fact that the announcement of Jesus' birth was made to shepherds in the field rather than to the elite of Jerusalem.

"He has sent Me to heal the brokenhearted," Isaiah's prophecy continues. This refers not so much to those who are emotionally despondent, but primarily to those who are brokenhearted over sin, those "who sigh and cry over all the abominations that are done" (Eze. 9:4). They are the same ones of whom Jesus said, "Blessed are those who mourn, for they shall be comforted" (Matt. 5:4).

"To preach liberty to the captives." The term here is reminiscent of the year of jubilee. As outlined in Leviticus, after a series of seven seven-year periods, the children of Israel were to celebrate the fiftieth year as a year of release. Sometimes, because of financial emergency, a landowner might find it necessary to sell his property or even himself. But at jubilee all lands reverted to their original owners, and all bonded servants regained their personal liberty.

Paul points out that sin makes slaves of us (Rom. 8:21). That is just the opposite of what Eve thought she would step into by partaking of the forbidden fruit. The serpent told her she would become like God; instead, she became Satan's plaything. Nevertheless, Satan relentlessly portrayed God as a tyrant.

Through the centuries Satan magnified his hold on the human race. By the time Jesus came to earth "the deception of sin had reached its height. All the agencies for depraving the souls of men had been put in operation.

"The Son of God, looking upon the world, beheld suffering and misery. With pity He saw how men had become victims of satanic cruelty. He looked with compassion upon those who were being corrupted, murdered, and lost. They had chosen a ruler who chained them to his car as captives. Bewildered and deceived, they were moving on in gloomy procession toward eternal ruin—to death in which is no hope of life, toward night to which comes no morning. Satanic agencies were incorporated with men. The bodies of human beings, made for the dwelling place of God, had become the habitation of demons. The senses, the nerves, the passions, the organs of men, were worked by supernatural agencies in the indulgence of the vilest lust. The very stamp of demons was impressed upon the countenances of men. Human faces reflected the expression of the legions of evil with which they were possessed.

"Such was the prospects upon which the world's Redeemer looked. What a spectacle for Infinite Purity to behold!" (*The Desire of Ages*, p. 36).

In reality, Israel was without excuse in having lost sight of God's character. Again and again He revealed Himself. To Moses in the wilderness God had described Himself in positive terms: "The Lord, the Lord God, merciful and gracious, long-suffering, and abounding in goodness and truth, keeping mercy for thousands, forgiving iniquity and transgression and sin" (Ex. 34:6, 7).

Years later the psalmist picked up on this theme: "For You, Lord, are good, and ready to forgive, and abundant in mercy to all those who call upon You" (Ps. 86:5).

Isaiah wrote: "I will mention the lovingkindnesses of the Lord and the praises of the Lord, according to all that the Lord has bestowed on us. . . . In all their affliction He was afflicted, and the Angel of His Presence saved them; in His love and in His pity He redeemed them; and He bore them and carried them all the days of old" (Isa. 63:7-9).

Jesus came to set the captives free. "Jesus said to those Jews who believed Him, 'If you abide in My word, you are My disciples indeed. And you shall know the truth, and the truth shall make you free.' They answered Him, 'We are Abraham's descendants, and have never been in bondage to anyone. How can you say, "You will be made free"?' Jesus answered them, 'Most assuredly, I say to you, whoever commits sin is a slave of sin. And a slave does not abide in the house forever, but a son abides forever. Therefore if the Son makes you free, you shall be free indeed'" (John 8:31-36).

Isaiah 42 closely parallels the sixty-first chapter. "Behold! My Servant whom I uphold, My Elect One in whom My soul delights! I have put My Spirit upon Him; He will bring forth justice to the Gentiles. He will not cry out, nor raise His voice, nor cause His voice to be heard in the street. A bruised reed He will not break, and smoking flax He will not quench; He will bring forth justice for truth. He will not fail nor be discouraged, till He has established justice in the earth" (verses 1-4).

Here again is portrayed the concern the Messiah will have for His people. If there be any faith at all, He will nurture and tend it. He will contend for justice.

The Gospels often speak of Jesus' personal concern for people. "When He saw the multitudes, He was moved with compassion for them, because they were weary and scattered, like sheep having no shepherd" (Matt. 9:36). The Greek for compassion is translated literally "to have the bowels yearning." Jesus never saw a crowd as a "sea of faces." Each person was an individual to Him, with particular needs and concerns, and Jesus *cared.*

He had compassion on the 5,000 men, besides women and children, who followed Him into the wilderness on the far side of Galilee. His disciples seemed to think that if they were hungry, that was their concern—no one had invited them. But Jesus made it His concern. He fed them.

Similarly with individuals—two blind men (Matt. 20:34), a leper in Galilee (Mark 1:41), the widow of Nain (Luke 7:13), the demon-possessed man of Gadara (Mark 5:19).

And can we ever forget the picture of Jesus weeping at Lazarus' tomb? He did not worry personally about the loss of His friend—but He empathized in spirit with those who did feel loss.

Again, as Jesus, riding on a colt in what has been called His triumphal entry into Jerusalem, approached the city, the insuperable obstinacy of its people overcame Him. He foresaw the armies of Rome surrounding the city, beating down its walls, killing women and children. "As He drew near, He saw the city and wept over it, saying, 'If you had known, even you, especially in this your day, the things that make for your peace!'" (Luke 19:41, 42).

Jesus had met a similar obstinacy in that synagogue in Nazareth. As soon as He indicated that His message of freedom encompassed Gentiles as well as Jews, they turned on Him to kill Him. He slipped out of their grasp, but His compassion did not fail. He would give them one more opportunity. Later.

The
Good Shepherd

7

"He will feed His flock like a shepherd; He will gather the lambs with His arm, and carry them in His bosom, and gently lead those who are with young" (Isa. 40:11). Again we are indebted to Isaiah, the gospel prophet, for a beautiful picture of the kind of Messiah God in His grace would provide His people.

Isaiah was not the first to use the metaphor of shepherd to describe the coming Redeemer, although his portrayal is the most colorful. (As mentioned earlier, Isaiah had an unsurpassed way with words.) On his deathbed Jacob had directed the attention of his sons to God. He "has fed me all my life long to this day," he said (Gen. 48:15). He is "the Shepherd, the Stone of Israel" (Gen. 49:24).

This would be a natural metaphor for Jacob to use, himself a shepherd, patriarch of a tribe of shepherds. But what about us, who live in a highly urbanized, mechanized society? Not many of us have had much firsthand experience in the natural world, the world of plants and animals, the outdoors. What do we have in common with sheep and shepherds? Can we find meaning in these terms?

Shall we search for some more relevant analogy—rewrite the Scriptures to fit our situation? It would be better to learn more of the natural world, where so much of Scripture language is couched—that world was here first, before the world of glass and steel. It is also closer to God's original work. We can learn better from the "original language." Perhaps we cannot study the Bible in Greek and Hebrew, but we can learn from "God's other book," the book of nature.

There is no harm in looking for a modern counterpart to the shepherd-sheep analogy, but if we find one, let us add it to the scriptural picture, not throw out the latter altogether. We have not bettered ourselves with our modern trappings; we would all benefit from harking back to simpler times, at least in matters of spirit. We cannot find in machinery and technology the personal and private insights that the Scriptures have provided from the natural world. So let us continue examining the shepherd theme.

David used the expression often. Referring to the exodus experience of his people from Egypt, David said of God: "He made His own people go forth like sheep, and guided them in the wilderness like a flock; and He led them on safely, so that they did not fear" (Ps. 78:52, 53). "You led Your people like a flock by the hand of Moses and Aaron" (Ps. 77:20).

Through Jeremiah and Ezekiel God carried on the figure. " 'I will gather the remnant of My flock out of all countries where I have driven them, and bring them back to their folds; and they shall be fruitful and increase. I will set up shepherds over them who will feed them; and they shall fear no more, nor be dismayed, nor shall they be lacking,' says the Lord" (Jer. 23:3, 4).

"I will establish one shepherd over them, and he shall feed them—My servant David. He shall feed them and be their shepherd" (Eze. 34:23). Of course, this was several generations after David; God referred here to the Messiah, who would come, as promised, in the line of David.

Aside from the fact that sheep were common in Israel and the other lands of the Bible, what is there about the sheep-shepherd relationship that renders it so valuable as a spiritual object lesson? A strong hint is given in the fifty-third chapter of Isaiah, which we referred to in the fifth chapter of this book. There the prophet says, "All we like sheep have gone astray; we have turned, every one, to his own way" (verse 6).

According to Phillip Keller, author of *A Shepherd Looks at Psalm 23,* sheep require more attention than any other livestock. In much of the world—including Palestine—their habitat consists of wild territory, full of natural predators, dangerous terrain, uncertain pasturage. In the face of these dangers, sheep are extremely vulnerable, with no means of protecting themselves. To top it all off, they are among the most perverse of domesticated creatures. The same sheep can get into the same predicament several times a day. And the whole flock is quick to follow the first sheep into the same danger.

The corollary is that the work of a shepherd is one of the most strenuous. Sheep will eat almost anything, and they have a habit of cropping plants close to the ground, even tearing up the roots if there is no other food. That means the shepherd must keep them on the move—no more than a week in one spot, or they will ruin the pasture for months or even years to come. So he must know where to take them next.

And he must know what dangers lurk—wild animals, snakes, poisonous plants. The sheep must have access to water—calm water, if it is running. Then there is danger from brambles, where the sheep might get hung up. There is danger from steep terrain, because domestic sheep do not have the agility to negotiate rough country that mountain sheep have.

The shepherd-psalmist asks, "Why art thou cast down, O my soul? and why art thou disquieted within me?" (Ps. 42:11, KJV). Shepherds speak of sheep as "cast" when they are down and cannot get back up. If fat, or heavy with lamb, or carrying a load of heavy wool, sheep can lose their balance. Once on their backs, they cannot right themselves. Gasses build up in their rumen. Blood circulation to the extremities is retarded. If the weather is hot, the sheep can die within a few hours.

Insects are a constant threat to sheep. Nasal flies will bite into the membrane of the nose and lay their eggs. When the larvae hatch, they burrow their way up into the sinuses, the eyes, and the brain of the sheep. The pain and irritation can drive the sheep to distraction, and they lose interest in eating and resting. They may even kill themselves in desperation.

Lambing is an especially stressful time for the shepherd, even with flocks that are carefully pastured within fences. Ewes will lamb at any time of day or night. Often the shepherd must give a hand in direct assistance to the process. Particularly he or she has to take care that the lamb finds and bonds with its mother. A ewe will not accept a lamb not her own; if there are twins or triplets—which is not unusual—one or more may have a hard time finding the mother. If the shepherd cannot get them together quickly, he or she may have to raise the lamb, not an easy task if there are many of them.

It takes a dedicated shepherd to put up with all these problems—not to mention the loneliness, the hardships of weather, the never-ending responsibility. Not surprisingly, from these shared experiences the sheep and the shepherd experience their own bonding. That is, if the shepherd really cares about the sheep.

Shepherding goes along with a certain type of personality. If the shepherd does not have it already, he or she acquires it in the work. Patience. Tenderness. Tenacity. Considerateness. Moses was impetuous after 28 years in Pharaoh's palace. He was not ready to lead Israel out of Egypt, but after 40 years in Midian spent caring for sheep, he was different.

Why were shepherds chosen to be the first recipients of the glad tidings of the Redeemer's birth? Was it because they were teachable, open to the ministrations of the Spirit? Was it because they would not be put off by finding the long-awaited Messiah-Prince in a lowly manger?

The Bible constantly contrasts between good shepherds and bad shepherds. The prophecies about the Messiah-Shepherd emphasize His caring nature. "The mountains shall depart and the hills be removed, but My kindness shall not depart from you, nor shall My covenant of peace be removed" (Isa. 54:10). " 'Comfort, yes, comfort My people!' says your God" (Isa. 40:1).

Bad shepherds do not care about the flock; they have their interest somewhere else. They may be hired to do the job, but they do not have their heart in it. God said to Ezekiel, "Prophesy against the shepherds of Israel, . . . 'Woe to the shepherds of Israel who feed themselves! Should not the shepherds feed the flocks? You eat the fat and clothe yourselves with the wool; you slaughter the fatlings, but you do not feed the flock'" (Eze. 34:2, 3).

In her book *In Pastures Green,* Bev Condy describes her experiences in raising a small herd of black Lincoln-Corriedale crossbred sheep, and the spiritual lessons she gained. A fellow sheep raiser had a ewe that had lost her udder because of mastitis. Without an udder the ewe could not properly care for lambs and should not have been bred. But the careless owner allowed that to happen.

He promised a neighbor she could have the lambs when they came—but he failed to notify her of the birth until 15 hours later. Newborn lambs must have colostrum—the first milk secreted by the mother after delivery. It provides strength, antibodies, vitamins, and protein. (Fortunately, the neighbor had some frozen colostrum on hand and was able to save the lambs.) That owner's crassness lowered his esteem in the eyes of his neighbors for miles around.

One day in Jerusalem Jesus healed a man who had been blind from birth. The remarkable incident came to the attention of the religious leaders. When they asked him who had made him to see and he identified Jesus as the benefactor, they disfellowshipped him! And they wanted to do the same with Jesus!

Jesus immediately made the matter the subject of a sermon about good shepherds and bad shepherds. "Most assuredly, I say to you, he who does not enter the sheepfold by the door, but climbs up some other way, the same is a thief and a robber. But he who enters by the door is the shepherd of the sheep. To him the door-keeper opens, and the sheep hear his voice; and he calls his own sheep by name and leads them out" (John 10:1-3).

The religious leaders did not get the drift of Jesus' words, so He put it more plainly: "I am the door. . . . If anyone enters by Me, he will be saved, and will go in and out and find pasture. The thief does not come except to steal, and to kill, and to destroy"—just like you would do to this man who was blind, and to Me—"I have come that they may have life, and that they may have it more abundantly" (verses 7-10).

Then Jesus said plainly, "I am the good shepherd." The religious leaders, who should have been shepherds, were robbing the sheep. They had ignored the door of grace that God had opened. They were bent on taking, and taking, and taking. Jesus came to give—to give His life, to give salvation.

Jesus went on. "And other sheep I have which are not of this fold; them also I must bring, and they will hear My voice; and there will be one flock and one shepherd" (verse 16). Jesus was speaking of the Gentiles. They were to be brought into the fold of the covenant, the fold of salvation.

Right there Jesus gave proof of His Messiahship, proof that He was the good shepherd of Isaiah's prophecy.

More clearly than any other prophet, Isaiah had seen that the Messiah would be the Saviour of all peoples, not just the Jews. "Behold! My Servant whom I uphold, My Elect One in whom My soul delights! I have put my Spirit upon Him; He will bring forth justice to the Gentiles" (Isa. 42:1). But when Jesus appeared on earth, no one among the Jews was ready to accept that concept. It was as much as a man's life was worth to even mention such an idea—Jesus had experienced something of that kind of wrath in His hometown. To declare it in Jerusalem, in the Temple itself, was signing His own death warrant.

But that was how He would accomplish His mission. The "one flock" that He envisioned would be the result of His laying down His life and taking it up again. The Shepherd would give His life for the sheep. That was implicit in the blood covenant God had made with Abraham. "Now may the God of peace who brought up our Lord Jesus from the dead, that great Shepherd of the sheep, through the blood of the everlasting covenant, make you complete in every good work to do His will, working in you what is well pleasing in His sight, through Jesus Christ, to whom be glory forever and ever. Amen" (Heb. 13:20, 21).

This is why the twenty-third psalm is so precious to us. Jesus is *our* Shepherd, too—not just David's, not just the Jews'. In *The Shepherd and His Sheep,* J. Walter Rich tells of a Christian traveler in Switzerland who came across an uneducated little shepherd boy. He told the boy about Jesus and taught him the first five words of the Shepherd Psalm: "The Lord is my Shepherd." He had the boy count off the words on his fingers.

Later the traveler returned by the same route and asked for the little boy. His mother replied that her son had died. "But if you are the one who taught him about the Good Shepherd, he wanted you to know that he died holding his fourth finger."

The same source quotes a Mrs. John R. Mott for the following perceptive observation:

"I shall not want rest. 'He maketh me to lie down in green pastures.'

"I shall not want drink. 'He leadeth me beside the still waters.'

"I shall not want forgiveness. 'He restoreth my soul.'

"I shall not want guidance. 'He leadeth me in the paths of

righteousness for his name's sake.'

"I shall not want companionship. 'Yea, though I walk through the valley of the shadow of death, I will fear no evil: for thou art with me.'

"I shall not want comfort. 'Thy rod and thy staff they comfort me.'

"I shall not want food. 'Thou preparest a table before me in the presence of mine enemies.'

"I shall not want joy. 'Thou anointest my head with oil.'

"I shall not want anything. 'My cup runneth over.'

"I shall not want anything in this life. 'Surely goodness and mercy shall follow me all the days of my life.'

"I shall not want anything in eternity. 'I will dwell in the house of the Lord forever.'

"That is what David said he would find in the Good Shepherd. And one day it occurred to me how this psalm was fulfilled in Christ. This is what I found in Christ's own words:

" 'I am the good shepherd.'

"Thou shalt not want rest. 'Come unto me, all ye that labour and are heavy laden, and I will give you rest.'

"Thou shalt not want drink. 'If any man thirst, let him come unto me, and drink.'

"Thou shalt not want forgiveness. 'The Son of man hath power on earth to forgive sins.'

"Thou shalt not want guidance. 'I am the way, the truth, and the life.'

"Thou shalt not want companionship. 'Lo, I am with you alway.'

"Thou shalt not want comfort. 'The Father . . . shall give you another Comforter.'

"Thou shalt not want food. 'I am the bread of life: he that cometh to me shall never hunger.'

"Thou shalt not want joy. 'That my joy might remain in you, and that your joy might be full.'

"Thou shalt not want anything. 'Whatsoever ye shall ask of the Father in my name, he may give it you.'

"Thou shalt not want anything in this life. 'Seek ye first the kingdom of God, and his righteousness; and all these things shall be added unto you.'

"Thou shalt not want anything in eternity. 'I go and prepare a place for you, . . . that where I am, there ye may be also.'"

How is it with you, my friend? Can you say with the little shepherd boy, "The Lord is *my* shepherd"?

The
Larger Circle

8

"He drew a circle that shut me out—
Heretic, rebel, a thing to flout.
But Love and I had the wit to win:
We drew a circle that took him in."
—"Outwitted," Edwin Markham

Why did Isaiah note so often that the Gentiles would be included in the mystery of divine grace? Of royal blood himself, he had instant access to the king of Judah. He knew of the goings and comings of royal messengers. He was well aware of the political currents of his day, at home and in other lands. Perhaps as a court personage he had a more cosmopolitan outlook than other prophets?

That is a possible reason, yet there were other prophets high in government, or at least with ready access to royal secrets, who did not make so many references to Gentiles being saved as Isaiah did. Daniel, Ezra, and Nehemiah come to mind.

Isaiah's concern for the non-Jew no doubt stemmed from the same source as his prophecies—God's Holy Spirit. Note some of these passages about the Messiah from the gospel prophet's pen:

"I, the Lord, have called You in righteousness, and will hold Your hand; I will keep You and give You as a covenant to the people, as a light to the Gentiles" (Isa. 42:6).

"Look to Me, and be saved, all you ends of the earth! For I am God, and there is no other" (Isa. 45:22).

"It is too small a thing that You should be My Servant to raise up the tribes of Jacob, and to restore the preserved ones of Israel; I will also give You as a light to the Gentiles, that You should be My salvation to the ends of the earth" (Isa. 49:6).

Notice especially this passage: "Also the sons of the foreigner who join themselves to the Lord, to serve Him, and to love the name of the Lord, to be His servants—everyone who keeps from defiling the Sabbath, and holds fast My covenant—even them I will bring to My holy mountain, and make them joyful in My house of prayer. Their burnt offerings and their sacrifices will be accepted on My altar; for My house shall be called a house of prayer for all nations" (Isa. 56:6, 7). We will have occasion to recall these words.

Why does it seem such a big thing to Isaiah that God would make His mercy and grace available to all peoples, nations, and tongues? After all, the original promise of salvation was made to the parents of the race. As in Adam all people have sinned, so in the promise to Adam all people have hope.

Sin threw up a barrier between mankind and God. Sin changed men and women, but it did not change God. Sin has limited God's contacts—His lines of communication with—human beings, but it has not altered His attitude toward His creatures.

Satan will do anything and everything to distort the Creator-creature relationship. On the one hand he will portray God as too far removed from our lives, then he will turn around and picture God as too involved, too dictatorial, too demanding. Or he will say God is stern, forbidding, daring us to disobey so that He can destroy us. If we don't go for that, Satan will try to picture God as easygoing, all-forgiving, a "pushover"—we can get by with anything.

When Jesus came to earth, the Jews considered themselves the one and only race deserving salvation. But it hadn't always been that way. At one time they had been severely taken to task for mingling too freely with the heathen nations around them. They had swung from one extreme to the other.

At a time when practically the whole world was taken up with idolatry, God had appeared to Abram. God wanted to establish a foothold, a beachhead, on this planet, from which He could reach out to all those who were not listening to Him. Calling Abram to separate himself from the pull of idolatrous kinfolk, God promised He would bless Abram—and make him a blessing to the nations around him (Gen. 12:1-3). In this first covenant with the father of the Hebrew race, God had indicated that His plans included all peoples.

As the children of Abraham, the Israelites, lodged in the wilderness on their way from Egypt to Canaan, God told them He would renew with them the covenant He had made with their father Abraham. They would be a distinct people, with special privileges. But this was not because they were of more inherent worth than the nations around them. Rather, they were to be a showcase to those nations, a living demonstration of what obedience and loyalty to God could bring to anyone. The Jewish nation was to be an avenue, an entering point, by which God could gain access to the rest of the world.

But Satan was ever ready with his devious ways. If he could not get them to fraternize with the heathen, he would get them to isolate themselves to the point of exclusion. Either way, they would fail in their commission to demonstrate God's abiding grace for all peoples.

Though few and far between, there were some notable points at which God was successful in reaching non-Jews. Rahab was a prostitute of Jericho. When stories of Israel's God preceded their advancing armies, she determined to throw in her lot with that people. As the city fell, she and her family were spared. They became a part of God's people.

King Solomon had the nations around Judah in mind when he built the beautiful Temple in Jerusalem. He looked for the day when they would come to this site to worship the true God. When he dedicated the edifice to the worship of God, he prayed: "Moreover, concerning a foreigner, who is not of Your people Israel, but has come from a far country for Your name's sake (for they will hear of Your great name and Your strong hand and Your outstretched arm), when he comes and prays toward this temple, hear in heaven Your dwelling place, and do according to all for which the foreigner calls to You, that all peoples of the earth may know Your name and fear You" (1 Kings 8:41-43).

And it did not take long for his prayer to be answered. The queen of Sheba "heard of the fame of Solomon concerning the name of the Lord" (1 Kings 10:1). After visiting him and studying with him, she gave God the glory for all she had seen: "Blessed be the Lord your God, who delighted in you. . . . Because the Lord has loved Israel forever, therefore He made you king" (verse 9).

Naaman was another foreign dignitary converted to the worship of the God of Israel. After having been healed of leprosy, he declared: "Now I know that there is no God in all the earth, except in Israel" (2 Kings 5:15).

Then we come to the story of Jonah, a rather paradoxical prophet. God called him to preach judgment against the city of Nineveh, capital of the Assyrians, but Jonah ran in the other direction. His flight was arrested by a storm at sea. Cast out of the ship and swallowed by a fish, he eventually came round to do the Lord's bidding.

"Yet forty days, and Nineveh shall be overthrown!" he proclaimed. The dirge had immediate effect. All these heathen people, right up to the king himself, repented and called on God's mercy. God called off the threatened judgment, and Jonah was furious. In his cutting remarks to God, Jonah's true motivation comes to light. In his insularism, he had resented God's interest in non-Jewish people. *Why go and warn this Gentile city?* he had reasoned. *Why give them a chance? Go ahead, God; strike them down without advance notice! Why should I go out of my way to help them?* Then when they repented and God did not destroy them, that was the last straw. God had missed His chance—and made Jonah look bad in the bargain.

In His reply to Jonah, God indicated that His love for mankind extended beyond Judah's borders: "Should I not pity Nineveh, that great city?" He asked (Jonah 4:11).

Contrarily, the people of the promise seemed to have no qualms about joining their neighbors in idolatry. But as for winning them to the religion of the true God, they fell woefully inadequate. They could go out and join their neighbors in sin, but they were too much "God's chosen people" to tell them about His saving grace.

Does that sound familiar? Many Christians today are more at ease in joining their godless friends in frivolity and games than in sharing their faith.

The 10 tribes of Israel fell more and more into idolatrous

ways, until God allowed the Assyrians to come and decimate them. Many were slain; the rest were chained and taken off into exile. For a while the two tribes of Judah avoided divine retribution. But eventually they, too, were carried into captivity, leaving their city and temple in ruins.

After 70 years, God allowed the Jews to return to their homeland. They began to rebuild Jerusalem, and especially the Temple. Then came word to their spiritual leader, Ezra, that the people were intermarrying with their pagan neighbors again. This was the very thing that had begun their slide into apostasy before. The news made Ezra visibly upset. Fortunately, the people themselves came up with the remedy—they put away their heathen wives.

But that was not the end of it. A few years later, when Nehemiah was governor, the same situation came to light again. It made Nehemiah very angry. He "contended with them and cursed them, struck some of them and pulled out their hair" (Neh. 13:25). "Did not Solomon king of Israel sin by these things?" he asked. "Pagan women caused even him to sin. Should we then hear of your doing all this great evil, transgressing against our God by marrying pagan women?" (verses 26, 27).

That seems to be the low point of Israel's fraternizing with nonbelievers. They swung the other way, to the other extreme. They came to the point where they would have as little as possible to do with anyone who was not a Jew. They despised their neighbors the Samaritans, and were sure God had no use for the Gentiles. For certain, they did not.

God still desired that the children of Israel, heirs of the promise to Abraham, should evangelize the world. " 'Return, O backsliding children,' says the Lord; 'for I am married to you. I will take you, . . . and I will bring you to Zion. . . . At that time Jerusalem shall be called The Throne of the Lord, and all the nations shall be gathered to it' " (Jer. 3:14-17).

"This promise of blessing [the promise to Abraham] should have met fulfillment in large measure during the centuries following the return of the Israelites from the lands of their captivity. It was God's design that the whole earth be prepared for the first advent of Christ, even as today the way is preparing for His second coming" *(Prophets and Kings*, pp. 703, 704).

But it was not to be.

Every time Jesus made an overture to non-Jews He was looked at askance—or worse. His disciples did not understand His actions, and His enemies used each occasion to build their case against Him. The first instance we have on record was His conversation with the Samaritan woman at Jacob's well.

"The stay of Jesus in Samaria was designed to be a blessing to His disciples, who were still under the influence of Jewish bigotry. They felt that loyalty to their own nation required them to cherish enmity toward the Samaritans. They wondered at the conduct of Jesus. . . . They were slow to learn that their contempt and hatred must give place to pity and sympathy. . . .

"The Saviour is still carrying forward the same work as when He proffered the water of life to the woman of Samaria. Those who call themselves His followers may despise and shun the outcast ones; but no circumstances of birth or nationality, no condition of life, can turn away His love from the children of men. To every soul, however sinful, Jesus says, If thou hadst asked of Me, I would have given thee living water" *(The Desire of Ages,* pp. 193, 194).

We have already noted (chapter 6) that in Jesus' discourse in the synagogue at Nazareth, it was not His claim to the fulfillment of Isaiah's prophecy of the Messiah that infuriated His listeners, but His inclusion of non-Jews in the kingdom of grace.

But that did not deter Him from pursuing His egalitarian ministry. His visit to Phoenicia was for the express purpose of healing the daughter of a woman from that area and the lesson that would teach His disciples. "This act opened the minds of the disciples more fully to the labor that lay before them among the Gentiles" *(ibid.,* p. 402). And note this: "The same agencies that barred men away from Christ eighteen hundred years ago are at work today. The spirit which built up the partition wall between Jew and Gentile is still active. Pride and prejudice have built strong walls of separation between different classes of men. . . .

"Caste is hateful to God. He ignores everything of this character. In His sight the souls of all men are of equal value" *(ibid.,* p. 403).

Later Jesus went to Jerusalem and the Temple there. This place had been ordained of God not only as the focal point for the Jews' worship but also as a means of attracting and instructing non-Jews in the ways of the Creator/Redeemer. (See *The Desire of Ages,* p. 161.) Yet a wall had been built around it, bearing an inscription explicitly forbidding Gentiles from approaching. Moreover, the system of offerings had become so commercialized that the poor among the Jews themselves could not afford to worship.

For the second time in His ministry, Jesus drove out the money changers, the livestock salesmen, the greedy priests. "Is it not written," He said in trumpet tones, " 'My house shall be called a house of prayer for all nations'? But you have made it a 'den of thieves' " (Mark 11:17).

In this one statement Jesus claimed the Messianic prophecy of Isaiah for Himself, and He reasserted the universality of His kingdom.

Note the progression of Jesus' revelations. In extending His grace to the Samaritans He had raised eyebrows, but with a stretch the liberal-minded could accept that, inasmuch as the Samaritans did consider Abraham their father and worshiped the true God, albeit not at Jerusalem. He took His message a step further by including the Gentile Phoenician woman. But now He was in the Temple, the very citadel of Jewishness—and He said that the Temple should be "a house of prayer for all nations."

After Jesus' resurrection and ascension, His disciples gradually came to understand the significance of those words, and similar ones He had used before. Philip went to Samaria and had great evangelistic success there. Soon after, Peter had a vision of a sheet let down from heaven, containing all kinds of unclean animals. The upshot of this vision, and the subsequent conversion of the Roman centurion Cornelius, was that Peter, and thence the rest of the apostles, realized that the gospel of grace was not to be limited to Jews. Saul (Paul) and Barnabas began their overt ministry to the Gentiles.

From the start Paul recognized he had been given a special commission to evangelize Gentiles. Whenever he came to a town for the first time, he began working among the Jewish population—after all, they had the background of the prophecies and could more quickly grasp how they were fulfilled in Jesus. But Paul usually found his most fruitful field among the Gentiles.

In introducing his God to the Greeks of the Areopagus (Mars' Hill), Paul described Him as the One "who made the world and everything in it" (Acts 17:24). "And He has made from one blood every nation of men to dwell on all the face of the earth, . . . so that they should seek the Lord, in the hope that they might grope for Him and find Him, though He is not far from each one of us" (verse 26).

Our study has come full circle. We have seen how the Israelites, the children of the covenant, took an offer of specialness and twisted it into exclusiveness. The same tendency, manifest in various forms of prejudice and insularism, permeates society today. But Isaiah's message rings down to our time: "Your Redeemer is the Holy One of Israel; He is called the God of the whole earth" (Isa. 54:5).

Or, as Paul concludes: "There is neither Jew nor Greek, there is neither slave nor free, there is neither male nor female; for you are all one in Christ Jesus" (Gal. 3:28).

God's
Twin Sisters

9

Conscientious writers—and speakers—are becoming more careful of the terms they use when they refer to people in general. Time was when such words as "men" and "he" could be used to imply people of either gender. But people's thinking changes, and language changes with it. Now careful communicators try to use "inclusive language," terms that are not gender-specific.

The committee that developed *The Seventh-day Adventist Hymnal* addressed this issue. The hymn "Rise Up, O Church of God" (No. 615) is a case in point. As originally written, the hymn was titled "Rise Up, O Men of God." Other phrases throughout the hymn also indicated that the words were addressed to only one gender—as indeed, the author had intended it. The hymnal committee liked the challenging message of the hymn as well as its music, but voted it down more than once because of its exclusiveness.

Finally, Ottilie Stafford, a member of the committee, discovered that a little rewriting could be done, the order of stanzas changed, and a stanza for youth added. Her version, which the committee happily accepted, includes both genders, and old and young as well! (Note: The hymn was in public domain, no longer under copyright, so the committee could do with it as they pleased.)

The editors at the Review and Herald® Publishing Association are similarly cognizant of the dangers of exclusive terminology. A sizable section of their stylebook gives guidance in how to write inclusively. The copy editors have also found help in *The Bias-*

Free Word Finder, by Rosalie Maggio, which deals specifically with the semantic problems that may be encountered.

But when it comes to inclusiveness, no one can outdo God. The very first chapter of the Bible indicates that when God incorporated His image in human form, it took both male and female humans to accomplish it. And God's first enunciation of the plan of salvation included the role that womanhood would play in His purpose.

Inclusiveness is also the message that comes across most clearly in Matthew's genealogy of Jesus Christ, and this has to do with more than just gender discrepancy. Compare Matthew's genealogy (Matt. 1) with Luke's (Luke 3). While Matthew does not go so far back as Luke, he does make some odd inclusions. Why? Perhaps the answer is in verse 21: "You shall call His name Jesus, for He will save His people from their sins." Matthew was illustrating—right in his genealogy—the truth of that statement. Many of the people in that list are known best by their sins!

We recognize, of course, that Jesus could not have been born into the human race without having sinners in His lineage, inasmuch as "all have sinned and fall short of the glory of God" (Rom. 3:23). Matthew was simply emphasizing that Jesus had sinners as well as saints in His ancestry. At the same time, Matthew was including everyone in God's saving grace.

Currently in the news are reports that some insurance companies have taken advantage of some of their customers. "The large print giveth, but the fine print taketh away." Some insurance salespeople promise things that the company will not deliver. (Of course, that happens in other types of business too.) But that is not the case with God's "assurance policy." He is "able to do exceedingly abundantly above all that we ask or think" (Eph. 3:20).

There is no sin so vile that it is not covered. Think of it: Could any sin be worse than Adam's simple bite of fruit? By that one disobedience Adam plunged the entire race into abject depravity. Nobody can sin worse than that. If God can forgive Adam, He can forgive anyone. We read, "God so loved the *world* that He gave His only begotten Son, that *whosoever* believes in Him should not perish but have everlasting life." You can't get more inclusive than that!

Of course, sometimes the problem is that we don't want to be included! We don't want to admit that we need salvation. We may not be perfect, but we're not all that bad—certainly not bad enough to warrant damnation! We all stretch our limits sometime, and God can stretch His. So we think.

And so thought the Pharisees of Jesus' day. But Jesus told them: "Those who are well have no need of a physician, but those who are sick. But go and learn what this means: 'I desire mercy and not sacrifice.' For I did not come to call the righteous, but sinners, to repentance" (Matt. 9:12, 13).

Who are the "righteous" Jesus might have called but didn't? Who are those who are "well"? *No one.* There are no such people. If we do not include ourselves among the "sick," if we do not recognize our need for the Great Physician, we place ourselves out in the cold. We write ourselves right out of heaven. If anyone is guilty of exclusiveness, it is human beings, not God.

Let's get back to that genealogy of Jesus. Let's see whom Matthew caught in his net. Abraham is called the father of the faithful, but Abraham's faith failed him at least twice—and on the very same point! In Egypt he told Pharaoh that Sarah was his sister. She was so beautiful that Abraham feared Pharaoh would kill him in order to get her. It took God's direct intervention to get him and Sarah out of that scrape (Gen. 12). Some 25 years later Abraham set himself up with the very same problem with Abimelech, a Philistine king. (Sarah was now 90 years old but still attractive!) Still, God kept renewing His covenant with Abraham so that the world's Redeemer would come through his line.

Then, would you believe it, Isaac tried the very same nefarious scheme with his wife, Rebekah—and involving Abimelech, too! It is enough to make one wonder what sort of concept the Philistine king had of the religion of Abraham's tribe that they should treat their neighbors so shabbily.

Jacob was an extremely shady character. Even his name, given because of an incident at birth, meant "supplanter" (to supplant means to cause to fall, or trip up through treachery). Jacob used his chicanery against his brother, Esau; against his blind father; and against his uncle Laban.

Next in Jesus' genealogy is Judah, Jacob's fourth son. Judah had three legitimate sons. He also had two sons, twins, by his daughter-in-law Tamar. She had disguised herself as a prostitute with the express purpose of becoming pregnant with Judah's child. (You can read the story in Genesis 38.) It was one of these illegitimate sons who continued the line of Jesus' ancestors.

Then come several progenitors of whom we know little or nothing. They represented the generations that grew up in Egypt. The next familiar name is that of Rahab. As Joshua, successor to Moses, prepared to invade Canaan with the children of Jacob, he sent two spies to Jericho to get a feel for the enemy he would be fighting. The spies chose to stay at the home of Rahab, a prostitute. This was not necessarily for entertainment purposes. It would not be unusual for strangers to be seen going and coming from her house, which was a part of the city wall. Also, people would be less likely to ask embarrassing questions of them in such a place, where privacy was to be expected.

Rahab went beyond giving the spies shelter. When the king of Jericho heard that enemy agents were at Rahab's house, he sent men to capture them. But Rahab realized that the days of Jericho were numbered. She recognized that the God of the Israelites would lead them to victory over Jericho. She put her own life at risk by hiding the spies; later she sent them away secretly.

Because of her lifestyle, God could justifiably have included Rahab among the slain of Jericho when the city was destroyed. But instead He rewarded her and all her relatives by delivering them, and that in a very spectacular way. Apparently her portion of the wall was the only part that remained intact when the rest came crashing down.

God also rewarded Rahab by putting her in the line of ancestors that would lead to the world's Saviour. And He honored her memory by having Matthew include her name in his list. Matthew could have written up the list without mentioning her, and he would have been perfectly in order in doing so. But there she is, right along with all those men's names.

Then we come to David. We have already noted some of David's many shortcomings, yet because of his quick and genuine repentance, God called him a "man after His own heart" (1 Sam. 13:14). But why should God choose, as David's spiritual heir, the son of an illicit affair? And why should Matthew go out of his way to point out Solomon's birth situation? To put the matter in today's vernacular, Matthew could have gone all day without bringing up the fact that Solomon was born by "her who had been the wife of Uriah."

Jesus could not have been born into the human race without having sinners in His family tree, but Matthew did not have to include references to Tamar and Rahab and Ruth (who, like Rahab, was not an Israelite), and Bathsheba. Including them in the sacred account is not an indication that God condoned their conduct. It *is* an indication that God's salvation is available to all people—men and women, Jews and Gentiles, and sinners of all stripes.

We have noted that some do not include themselves within the number of those needing God's grace. They do not recognize their sinfulness, and so, of course, they do not seek salvation. But it is just as dangerous to assume we are outside God's ability or willingness to save. To our adversary the devil it does not matter to which extreme we succumb. If we say we are not sinful enough or that we are too sinful, the result is the same—we cannot enter the kingdom of God.

This underscores the role that faith plays in our conversion. In Hebrews 11:6 we read: "Without faith it is impossible to please Him, for he who comes to God must believe that He is, and that He is a rewarder of those who diligently seek Him." It is our concept of God—of His majesty, of His holiness, of His right to rule—that brings us to repentance.

When we keep our eyes on ourselves, we become deceived about our own spiritual condition. When we catch a vision of God's character, we see ourselves in a true light and abhor ourselves. This first vision of God may concentrate on His judgment and justice. If we stop there in our investigation as to what God is like, we will fail to learn and experience His mercy. So we will have a one-sided understanding of God. We will either fear Him, afraid of His wrath, distrustful of His readiness to forgive us, or we will consider Him as lenient, one who does not take our sins seriously.

This is why continuous Bible study is so important. The stories and parables and even the prophecies of the Bible are interesting. If we are satisfied that we know them quite well, thank you, and can retell them at will, we may come to feel we are quite conversant with the Bible and do not need to continue studying it so much. But when we recognize how quickly we can deviate from the *principles* of those stories, when we see how readily we fall into one ditch or the other, that we are either not sinful enough or too sinful—then we will know our need for constant reality checks.

The dichotomous thinking that leads people to consider themselves as either too good to need salvation or too evil to be saved has a parallel in how God is seen. For some He is so loving and kind that He would never bring Himself to punish us, certainly not to the extent of death for the sinner. God even described Himself as "merciful and gracious, long-suffering, and abounding in goodness and truth, keeping mercy for thousands, forgiving iniquity and transgression and sin" (Ex. 34:6, 7).

Others see God as judgmental, more ready to condemn than to forgive. They remember that God put Adam and Eve out of the Garden of Eden, that He destroyed the earth and most of mankind with a flood, that He sent plagues to Egypt, and yes, to Israel in the wilderness. They remember that He struck down Uzzah simply for trying to steady the ark of the covenant when it jostled along a rough road.

Do we have a God of justice or of mercy? To us, these are opposites, but in God they are perfectly blended, balanced. In fact, they are both mentioned by God in that description of Himself quoted from Exodus 34 (see verse 7). His justice identifies and condemns sin; His mercy provides a way out. His mercy gives us hope; His justice gives us character.

An incident in the early history of Israel illustrates this. While Moses and Joshua were in the mountain receiving from God the Ten Commandments on tablets of stone, his people were down below making and worshiping a golden calf. Moses came down and caught them at the height of debauchery. After throwing down the tables of law and breaking them, Moses burned the calf and ground it to powder. Then he threw the residue into the supply of drinking water and made the people drink it. Finally, he called for the people to repent. Three thousand of the people stubbornly refused to repent of their sin. God instructed Moses to slay these diehards. Why?

"One bad apple can spoil the barrel." Had they continued to sin, God could not have protected them from their enemies in the wilderness. "It was the mercy of God that thousands should suffer, to prevent the necessity of visiting judgments upon millions" *(Patriarchs and Prophets,* p. 325). Further, had this sin been overlooked, when Israel reached Canaan they could not condemn idolatry among the Canaanites—and could not morally have disenfranchised them of the land.

In the Psalms we see these two apparently opposite characteristics, justice and mercy, coming together in God: "Will You be angry with us forever? Will You prolong Your anger to all generations? Will You not revive us again, that Your people may rejoice in You? Show us Your mercy, O Lord, and grant us Your salvation. I will hear what God the Lord will speak, for He will speak peace to His people and to His saints; but let them not turn back to folly. Surely His salvation is near to those who fear Him, that glory may dwell in our land. Mercy and truth have met together; righteousness and peace have kissed" (Ps. 85:5-10).

In William Shakespeare's *Merchant of Venice,* Portia emphasizes this point. She says of mercy: "It is enthroned in the hearts of kings, it is an attribute to God Himself; and earthly power doth then show likest God's, when mercy seasons justice."

It is in this sense that Ellen White refers to mercy and justice as "twin sisters" *(Testimonies,* vol. 4, pp. 209, 363, 420). It is the mixture of these two, the coworking of God's justice and mercy, that brings sinners to repentance *(ibid.,* vol. 2, p. 423). Without the one, we would not see our need to repent of sin; without the other, we would see no hope in doing so.

No wonder, then, that it is Satan's intense purpose to separate in our thinking God's mercy from His justice. The adversary would like us to get hung up on the one or the other, that God is too merciful to destroy sinners, or He is too bent on justice to allow sinners to live. But we have the promise in Hebrews 7:25: "He is also able to save to the uttermost those who come to God through Him, since He ever lives to make intercession for them."

And in his genealogy of Jesus, Matthew shows that we are all sinners—and Jesus came to save each one of us.

The Man Who Was Twice Blessed

10

Some 700 years had passed over the Land Between the Seas since Isaiah, the eloquent prophet, had detailed the coming of the Messiah. More than 500 years had transpired since Daniel had pinpointed the year when "the Messiah shall be cut off." Babylon, the golden empire that had carried the Jews into exile, had turned to dust. The silver of Persia had given way to the stronger bronze of Greece. Now the iron fist of Rome lay heavy on the land.

The new Temple in Jerusalem provided a focal point for those Jews scattered over the empire as well as those at home. City and Temple seethed with passion and intrigue. Pious worshipers, the professionally religious, Roman soldiers and politicos, toadies to the Romans, elitist Hellenists, treasonous plotters, merchants, travelers from foreign lands, and common people interested only in their immediate needs—all mixed and mingled in the narrow streets.

But no scion of David reigned in David's royal city. What had happened to the promises of a Branch of Jesse? Where was the Scepter of Judah? Although Daniel had seemed to be very exact in his prophecy of "sixty-two weeks" (and they understood that to mean weeks of years, or 434 years) "from the going forth of the command to restore and build Jerusalem until Messiah the Prince," the Jews did not know just what that entailed. Was that when He would overthrow the Romans, or when He would first appear on the political scene, or when He would be born?

And just how did Isaiah's prophecies about a Suffering Servant enter the picture? They chose to ignore that. Their

Messiah would cast off Roman rule and make Israel the center of the world. The end result of such a mental focus was less and less concentration on the Messiah and more and more on themselves.

To the north of Jerusalem and its province of Judea, separated from them by the notorious Samaritans, lay the province of Galilee. Popularly speaking, there were two Galilees, Upper and Lower. The Upper was to the north, but it was so called because its elevation was greater. It was also less populous.

Lower Galilee was relatively prosperous. Almost every industry known to humanity found a place there—agriculture, fishing, manufacturing, crafts, commerce. Especially commerce. Of course, north-and-south trade routes ran through the land, carrying goods and people from Egypt and Ethiopia to Asia Minor, Persia, and unknown lands beyond. In addition, three east-west routes connecting seaports on the Great Sea, the Mediterranean, with Damascus and the East passed through this province. If for any reason you were going any great distance—and you didn't want to chance the sea—at some point you found yourself in Galilee.

Josephus characterized the Galileans as impulsive, brave, straight-spoken. They also had a patois, a dialect, all their own. Judeans held them in contempt because of it, but the Galileans didn't mind. They prided themselves in their identity. More than nationalistic, they harbored sedition.

A valley piercing the hills of central Galilee from the south opened into an amphitheater circled by some 15 peaks. From the highest of these—only about 500 feet above the valley floor and some 1,600 feet in elevation above sea level—one could see the Mediterranean to the west. In the north loomed Mount Hermon and intervening lesser peaks.

On the slopes of this higher point of the amphitheater perched the village of Nazareth. Small but not insignificant, for it lay along the lower of the three trade routes to the East. Caravans of traders, travelers, and military troops found food and shelter among the inns and houses that terraced the hillside.

In one of those houses lived a widowed carpenter, Joseph by name, and his children. For whatever reason, Joseph was not wealthy; indeed, he was rather poor. But he was lonely, in spite of the children around his table. So he sought a wife, and he found her in the youthful Mary. Considering his financial circumstances, the dowry would not have been much, nor the betrothal ceremony elaborate. For the well-to-do, a public feast would be appropriate; for the poor, a simple statement in writing would be sufficient.

In Galilee at that time, more so than in Jerusalem, betrothal was as binding as the wedding ceremony and could be dissolved only by divorce proceedings. (This is still true in some parts of the world. In the Philippines a man told me that if someone were to break a wedding engagement to his daughter, he would kill him for infidelity.) Again, the divorce could be public or private. As long as two witnesses were present, a written statement would effect the dissolution. Of course, this power rested only in the husband; the wife could not initiate divorce.

But soon after the betrothal Mary disappeared. Joseph learned she had gone to the hill country south of Jerusalem to visit a relative. When she returned after an absence of three months, she confided in Joseph a secret. However thrilling the news might have been to her, it was a terrible blow to him: Mary, his betrothed, was pregnant—and had been since before her departure!

He was not the father, he knew. And he must have been surprised at what this situation said about Mary's character. He thought he knew her better than that.

He cast about as to what to do. Marry her anyway? But she was an adulteress; his own virtuous character rebelled against taking that kind of woman to his bosom. Besides, the truth about the real father could come out at any time, and he would be seen as a cuckold. He would have to break the betrothal, divorce her before they were married.

How should he divorce her? Publicly? Make a spectacle of her? It might boost his stock among his neighbors, let them see how pious he was. But it would devastate Mary, who probably was already suffering a lot of mental anguish. She would have enough trouble raising the child by herself. Besides, it was not Joseph's nature to hurt anyone or to seek gain for himself. He would divorce Mary quietly, with as little ado as possible. Just the two required witnesses—and they could be family members.

While Joseph wrestled on his bed with these thoughts, he had a dream. Now, for a Jew a dream was considered a mark of God's favor. In fact, the Jews recognized three "good things": a good king (it had been a long time since they had seen one of those—neither the Ceasars nor the Herods could qualify), a fruitful year (Joseph could have hoped for more along that line), and a good dream.

In his dream Joseph was addressed by an angel: "Joseph, son of David . . ." Why this form of greeting? There must have been many sons of David in Galilee that night. It really didn't signify much anymore.

But there *was* significance. In using that phrase the angel harked back to the covenant made with Israel's most illustrious king. "I will set up your seed after you," the Lord told David, "who will come from your body, and I will establish his kingdom. . . . Your throne shall be established forever" (2 Sam. 7:12-16). Only the Messiah could have an eternal reign. The Promised One would come through David's line. Joseph, son of Heli, was of that line.

Joseph had no illusions that he himself would be the Messiah. But there was a reason that the angel used that form of address . . .

The angel continued: "Do not be afraid to take to you Mary your wife, for that which is conceived in her is of the Holy Spirit. And she will bring forth a Son, and you shall call His name Jesus, for He will save His people from their sins" (Matt. 1:20, 21).

That was it! That was the answer to his dilemma! Now he knew why Mary was pregnant—sweet, chaste Mary. She hadn't been promiscuous—she had been visited by God! Now he knew what to do about her—he would marry her! Now he knew how and when the Messiah would join the human race. There were lots of things he didn't know, but he was satisfied.

Both Joseph and Mary were of the royal line of David. Herein is seen God's wisdom. Mary was the only human physically involved in the Messiah's birth. For the prophecy to be true, it was imperative that she be of the royal line. But Joseph was the "official" father, the one so registered in the synagogue. For the public record it was necessary that *he* have the appropriate lineage. God took care that both mother and "father" were children of David!

Surely the news of the Saviour was more startling to Joseph than what to do about Mary. The Messiah was to be not just a deliverer from Roman domination; His appearance meant more than just a return of the Davidic dynasty. The Messiah would be a

Saviour from sin! Release from eternal chains, not temporal ones!

Joseph had just been let in on the secret of the ages. Adam, Enoch, Abraham, Isaac, Jacob, Moses, David, Isaiah, Daniel, and many generations between and after had longed to see this day. How many prophecies, how many dreams, how many visions, had pointed to this moment? "Of this salvation the prophets have inquired and searched diligently, who prophesied of the grace that would come to you" (1 Peter 1:10). See how Joseph was twice blessed. He was a recipient of God's grace. How marvelous that God should transcend all barriers, the vast chasm between divinity and humanity, the distance between the Supreme Ruler of the universe and one of His poor subjects here on rebellious Earth! How wonderful that He should choose a humble carpenter as the human father of His Son! But then that is the essence of grace—the undeserved favor God bestows.

Joseph was also the channel of grace. Through him God would provide strength and protection for Mary and for the young Jesus. Through Joseph as surely as through Abraham, the whole world would be blessed.

Twice blessed—as a recipient of grace and as a channel of grace. But then, aren't we all twice blessed? The grace God extends to us is to serve as a pathway for others to come to Him. We are conduits for His blessings to the world around us.

How the priests and rulers in Jerusalem would have liked to know what Joseph knew—not that they would have believed as he believed. And therein is another wonderful thing about Joseph. Suppose he had passed off his dream as a figment of the imagination, the result of worrying too much about his situation, or perhaps the consequence of a bad meal? What would God have done had Joseph not been so ready to accept the message of His angel?

Abraham had been in a similar situation, though not fraught with so much eternal consequence. Yet Abraham's situation was to him more personally traumatic, perhaps, than Joseph's.

For years Abraham had been waiting for a son. Not only would a son carry on his name, but also God had promised that Abraham's descendants would possess the land of Canaan. In fact, the whole world would be blessed through One who came through his line. Abraham wanted to get on with it—he wanted a son! He had Ishmael by Hagar, but God told him that would not do. Finally, in her old age his wife Sarah bore Isaac. What a glory that boy was to his father! He could see the future in that son!

Then one night God told Abraham to offer Isaac as a burnt offering. No ifs, ands, or buts. No explanation. Just take the boy and slay him as a sacrifice, like an ordinary lamb would be offered.

How Abraham must have struggled with that order! Maybe he hadn't heard right. Maybe he had just had a nightmare that would fade with the dawn. Maybe it was Satan playing tricks on him.

But no, Abraham *knew that voice!* He had heard it before. He recognized God's voice. Being the man of faith that he was, Abraham obeyed. God honored his faith and provided a ram as a substitute sacrifice. The experience has been a lesson to every generation since. God means what He says—and it behooves us to know when He speaks to us.

Nehemiah had an experience the other way around. A man in a very responsible position to the Persian monarch Artaxerxes I, Nehemiah had gone to Jerusalem to help restore that city from its destruction under Nebuchadnezzar. But Sanballat, governor of a neighboring province, hated to see Jerusalem regain its prominence. First he tried to intimidate Nehemiah, and even to use force against him, but to no avail. Then he tried subterfuge.

Shemaiah, claiming to be a prophet of God, came to Nehemiah with what sounded like a spiritual message: "Let us meet together in the house of God, within the temple, and let us close the doors of the temple, for they are coming to kill you" (Neh. 6:10).

That sounds appropriate, doesn't it? What better place to hide from God's enemies than in God's house? But Nehemiah wasn't buying. First, to hide would indicate fear, and Nehemiah was not afraid. Second, he could not hide and still be doing God's will, which for him was to rebuild Jerusalem! Nehemiah recorded: "Then I perceived that God had not sent him at all, but that he pronounced this prophecy against me because Tobiah and Sanballat had hired him" (verse 12).

How did Abraham recognize God's voice? How did Nehemiah recognize that God was *not* speaking through Shemaiah? How do *we* recognize *anyone's* voice? Through association, through experience, through hearing it again and again. The more we study the

Bible, the more time we spend with God, letting Him talk to us through His Spirit, letting Him guide us in our lives and in specific situations, the more readily we can recognize His voice. Our salvation—and sometimes, in an emergency, our physical life—depends on it.

Jesus used a parable to bring home this lesson. "He who does not enter the sheepfold by the door, but climbs up some other way, the same is a thief and a robber. But he who enters by the door is the shepherd of the sheep. To him the doorkeeper opens, and the sheep hear his voice; and he calls his own sheep by name and leads them out. And when he brings out his own sheep, he goes before them; and the sheep follow him, for they know his voice" (John 10:1-4).

The picture is of a sheepfold, holding the flocks of several shepherds. When one shepherd calls, only his sheep come. They separate themselves from their fellows and follow their shepherd. The other sheep pay no attention to him. "I am the good shepherd," Jesus says, "and I know My sheep, and am known by My own" (verse 14).

It was in this way that Joseph knew that the angel who appeared to him in a dream was God's own messenger. Joseph, too, had had sufficient experience with God to know Him when he heard Him. And just this one thing about Joseph demonstrated that God had chosen wisely when He picked him out to be the earthly father of His Son. Not only would Joseph respond to this dream and accept Mary as his wife, but he would also obey the Holy Spirit's instructions in giving guidance to the growing Jesus.

Joseph lost no time in formally taking Mary as his wife. The earlier the better, as far as her reputation was concerned. (Luke speaks of Mary as Joseph's "betrothed"—the word "wife" does not appear in some ancient manuscripts—when they went to Bethlehem to register in Caesar's census. But they could not have traveled together had they not been really married. This simply demonstrates how "betrothal" and "marriage" carried similar weight.)

Three more times God had occasion to speak to Joseph. After the visit of the Wise Men to the infant Jesus, when Herod plotted to destroy all the babies of Bethlehem in order to preempt a threat to his throne, "an angel of the Lord appeared to Joseph in a dream, saying, 'Arise, take the young Child and His mother, flee to Egypt, and stay there until I bring you word; for Herod will seek the young Child to destroy Him'" (Matt. 2:13).

When Herod was dead, "an angel of the Lord appeared in a dream to Joseph in Egypt, saying, 'Arise, take the young Child and His mother, and go to the land of Israel, for those who sought the young Child's life are dead'" (verses 19, 20). (Who besides Herod was included in this statement? Who else was afraid of a coup? And wouldn't it be interesting to know if it was the same angel who appeared to Joseph in each dream? Or did God give different angels the privilege of conveying His messages concerning His Son?)

And finally, again in a dream, God warned Joseph not to settle in Judea. Back home, it was, to Nazareth. To that little hamlet on the hillside, perhaps to the same house and the same shop from where he and Mary had started out what seemed to be ages ago. So much had transpired in the meantime. What lay ahead?

Two Women,
Two Miracles

11

In chapter 1 we noted that grace is God's love demonstrated to us when we are unlovable, His favor extended to us when we don't merit it. He gives us more than we deserve. Grace is always "amazing" because that is not the way we humans are used to operating.

The all-pervading sin of mankind is to make ourselves out to be more than we really are. This does not refer to the laudable goal of self-improvement; it refers to the carnal tendency to self-exaltation. (What a fine line we draw here: what differentiates self-respect from self-honor? self-sufficiency from self-help?) We come by this tendency by nature—we are born that way, born of Adam and Eve, who passed it on to us. Eve's first sin was not in eating the forbidden fruit—it was in thinking she could make of herself a god.

The higher the opinion we have of ourselves, the less likely we are to recognize God's grace when it is manifested. The more self-sufficient we are, the less God can do for us. Every time in the Bible when we see people failing, it was because they tried to do their own thing. And every time in the Bible when we find someone spiritually successful, it was because he or she relied fully on the Lord.

The experiences surrounding Jesus' birth bring this lesson home to us.

To some, Zacharias was a pathetic figure. First, because he had no children. This was always a disaster in Jewish culture. Lineage and descent meant much to them. It gave them their place in society, their contribution to the welfare of the whole, and their claim to fellowship among the "people of the covenant." It also gave them title to land, and land was a part of the Abrahamic covenant (Gen. 15:7). Without children, Zacharias was little more than a zero.

Second, Zacharias made his home in the "hill country," the area of Judea south of Jerusalem. To the snobs in the capital, he lived in the sticks, in the boonies.

But Zacharias had one thing going for him—he was a priest. Inherent in that position he had the possibility of assisting in public worship at the Temple. But there were so many priests, and only one Temple, that they all had to take turns. This was determined by lottery, not only in how they would serve, but even in whether they would serve.

The Bible says Zacharias was "righteous before God, walking in all the commandments and ordinances of the Lord blameless" (Luke 1:6). This does not mean he never sinned; it means his heart was ever Godward. His intentions put God first; he did not cherish sin.

Zacharias had another good thing going for him—a good wife. Elizabeth was of the same character as her husband. She couldn't bear children, but she was faithful to her Lord. Like her husband, she was a direct descendant of the first priest of Israel, Aaron. In fact, she had the same name as Aaron's wife. Elizabeth and Zacharias had prayed for children until they had grown so old there was not much use to pray that prayer anymore.

The time came for Zacharias to fulfill his priestly duties at the Temple. Each day a lot would be cast as to who would offer the burnt offering, who would prepare the interior of the Holy Place, and who would offer the incense. The latter was the most exalted job of all. While the incense was offered, the worshipers outside were praying. The incense represented those prayers arising to God. The priest was making a pathway for their prayers to heaven.

Those chosen for the other tasks would serve at both morning and evening sacrifice, but the lot would be cast again to determine who would burn the evening incense. So honored was this position that no one could do it twice—once in a lifetime was enough. And Zacharias was chosen.

What was Zacharias thinking when he entered the sacred precincts, swinging his censer? Did he still have on his heart his life-long prayer for a son, or was he rejoicing in this one honor that he could carry to his grave? Or was he full of contrition, conscious that as a mortal man he really did not belong in the presence of the Holy?

Suddenly he realized he was not alone. A being stood beside the incense altar. Intuitively Zacharias knew it was an angel, and his heart seemed to jump into his throat. Was there something about his job that he was doing wrong? He had practiced often for its eventuality. Was there something in his personal life that forbade his presence here in this sacred place? His initial shock and fear were abated by the angel's first words: "Do not be afraid, Zacharias, for your prayer is heard; and your wife Elizabeth will bear you a son, and you shall call his name John" (verse 13).

Great as that news was, it kept getting better and better. This son would be "great in the sight of the Lord." He would be "filled with the Holy Spirit"—in Zacharias' familiarity with Scripture, that meant his son would be a prophet! But there was more: his son would go before the Lord "in the spirit and power of Elijah, . . . to make ready a people prepared for the Lord" (verses 14-17). This last phrase evoked the prophet Malachi's closing words, which had always been applied to the harbinger of the Promised One. Zacharias' son would introduce the Messiah!

This was more than the poor man could take. "How shall I know this?" he queried. As happens with so many of us today, Zacharias could not be satisfied with just the Lord's word—for surely he understood that the angel spoke for God. He wanted a sign. When will we learn that God's word is His power? When He speaks, worlds come into existence. "All His biddings are enablings" (*Christ's Object Lessons*, p. 333).

The angel looked at Zacharias sternly. "I am Gabriel," he said, "who stands in the presence of God" (verse 19). He gave Zacharias a sign as he asked, but it was also a punishment for his doubt: he would be dumb until the promise met its fulfillment.

Still, in all this God was demonstrating His grace. Not to the Sanhedrin did Gabriel appear, or to Annas the high priest. He did not show himself to any of the priests of Jerusalem, who looked down on the "rustic" from the hill country. They may have had the intellect and the training. They surely had more influence, power—and yes, wealth, ill-gotten though that may have been. But they did not have God's favor. "The Lord does not see as man sees; for man looks at the outward appearance, but the Lord looks at the heart" (1 Sam. 16:7).

Zacharias' loss of speech was of significance to others than Zacharias. The people who waited for him to come out of the Temple and wondered and perhaps worried at his delay saw that he had received a vision. Surely they soon learned the details. Then there were Elizabeth, her neighbors, and later Mary. They all learned that not only would the couple have a son in their old age, but also that he would usher in the golden age of the Messiah. Like Joseph would be, so Zacharias was a conduit of God's grace to others.

Luke leaves to the imagination how Zacharias broke the news to Elizabeth that she would be a mother at last. Probably he wrote out the account of his encounter with Gabriel. Also left to our imagination is Elizabeth's reaction to the news. Sometimes the women took their childlessness harder than the men—especially if it was known, as apparently it was in her case, that the cause lay with the wife.

Devout Elizabeth ascribed all praise to its rightful owner: "Thus the Lord has dealt with me, in the days when He looked on me, to take away my reproach among men" (Luke 1:25). Wisely she secluded herself for at least the first five months of her pregnancy. She would take no chance of miscarriage with such an important baby. God had done what she could not do, in helping her conceive; she would do what she could do, in vouchsafing His gift.

Gabriel's message to Zacharias did not reveal how long a time would intervene between the appearance of the King's herald and the coming of the King Himself. In reality, it was only six months until Gabriel made another trip from heaven's throne room to this rebellious but most favored planet. This time his destination was a humble cottage in a small town in an undistinguished province: Nazareth of Galilee, the home of Mary, a young woman whose parents were probably deceased (they are not mentioned at all in the sacred annals).

Abruptly Gabriel appeared before Mary in her home—in person, not in a dream as he later did to Joseph. Apparently she was not as shocked by his appearance as was Zacharias. (Perhaps hers was a more trusting nature? Perhaps Zacharias was more on edge because of the seriousness of his occupation?) "Rejoice, highly favored one," Gabriel greeted her. "The Lord is with you; blessed are you among women!" (verse 28).

Mary was more puzzled than frightened. "Highly favored"? "Blessed among women"? *Her?* She was just an ordinary maiden of an ordinary family in an ordinary town. Perhaps poorer than many. Yes, she was engaged to be married, but how did that make her "highly favored"? Joseph also was just a poor tradesman.

"Behold, you will conceive in your womb and bring forth a Son, and shall call His name Jesus," Gabriel explained. And as in his message to Zacharias, his words became progressively weightier as he went on. "He will be great, and will be called the Son of the Highest; and the Lord God will give Him the throne of His father David" (verses 31, 32). The Messiah? "And He will reign over the house of Jacob forever, and of His kingdom there will be no end" (verse 33). *The Messiah!*

Mary was almost speechless. Highly favored, indeed. Every generation since Eve had hoped to hear those words. Every Hebrew woman since Sarah had hoped to be the instrument to bring them about.

At last Mary found her voice. "How can this be, since I do not know a man?" (verse 34). There was no doubting here, as with Zacharias. She simply wanted to know the procedure. How could she cooperate? What was expected of her? What should she do?

"The Holy Spirit will come upon you," Gabriel explained, "and the power of the Highest will overshadow you; therefore, also, that Holy One who is to be born will be called the Son of God" (verse 35). Oh, how we wish Gabriel had been more specific! How many arguments have arisen in the Christian church because we don't know more of the details of that conception! But that is all we need to know. It is probably all we could understand even if more details had been given. This is a matter of divine action. At some point the human mind reaches its capacity to understand, and faith supplies the rest.

Gabriel indicated that nothing was required on Mary's part. It would be God's doing. The experience of Mary was analogous (though by no means identical) to our "new birth" as Christians. As we humble ourselves to the Spirit He "baptizes" (overshadows) us, and we become new creatures. We are reminded how at the very beginning of Creation the Spirit of God "hovered" over the waters. The Holy Spirit, as the breath of God, has always been the dynamic, the executing force, of the Godhead.

Mary did not ask for a sign of Gabriel's veracity, but he gave her one anyway. "Elizabeth your relative has also conceived a son in her old age" (verse 36). Would not Mary have known this already? Not necessarily. The Greek word rendered "cousin" in the King James Version does not carry the closeness of relationship that we know as cousin today. In addition, the relatively long distance between the two towns could preclude such news. Surely Gabriel would not have told Mary about Elizabeth in just those words if she had already known it.

The divine messenger concluded his visit with this cogent observation: "With God nothing is impossible."

How true! But how difficult it is for us to grasp and remember it! Forgetting that God can do everything, we try to do it all. But that leaves no room for God's grace.

Sometimes God puts us in a position where we *have* to recognize His hand. When Israel was oppressed by the Midianites, God called Gideon to lead His people to deliverance. Gideon recruited an army some 32,000 strong to fight a foe of 135,000. Ragtag his army was, with only a handful of weapons in the whole bunch (the Midianites had prevented them from even sharpening their own agricultural tools).

But the 32,000 were too many for God. He would work in their behalf—they hadn't been able to do it themselves. But with such a group they would take to themselves any credit for pushing out the Midianites. How well God knows us!

So at God's instructions, Gideon told everyone who was a bit fearful to go back home. Twenty-two thousand found themselves in that category! With a little experiment in human psychology at a brook, the 10,000 men were reduced to 300, and God said that was fine! They went on to rout the enemy.

Some centuries later Jehoshaphat, king of Judah, faced another horde, the combined armies of the Ammonites and the Moabites. Through a prophet God told the king, "You will not need to fight in this battle. Position yourselves, stand still and see the salvation of the Lord" (2 Chron. 20:17). The next morning Jehoshaphat encouraged his people, "Believe in the Lord your God, and you shall be established; believe His prophets, and you shall prosper" (verse 20). With those words, he put the *choir* at the head of his army and went to meet the enemy. When he came upon them, he found they had all killed each other.

Mary had all this and more to support her faith in Gabriel's words. She agreed, "with God, nothing will be impossible." "Behold the maidservant of the Lord!" she said. "Let it be to me according to your word" (Luke 1:37, 38).

Quickly Mary made her way to Elizabeth's house. She had to tell somebody, and she needed counsel. Apparently she had no close family, and she wasn't ready to tell Joseph yet! Besides, as a fellow recipient of God's grace, the elderly Elizabeth could understand her situation if anyone could.

At the sound of Mary's voice the 6-month-old fetus in Elizabeth's womb made a leap. The King's herald was welcoming the King! Under the power of the Holy Spirit, the godly Elizabeth recognized immediately the implications of the situation: "Blessed are you among women, and blessed is the fruit of your womb. [That was what the angel had said!] . . . Blessed is she who believed, for there will be a fulfillment of those things which were told her from the Lord" (verses 42-45).

Mary relaxed in the affirmation Elizabeth gave her, and she broke forth in song: "My soul magnifies the Lord, and my spirit has rejoiced in God my Savior" (verses 46, 47). She went on to echo the theme that God does indeed seek out the meek and lowly upon whom to bestow His favor, His grace. "He has put down the mighty from their thrones, and exalted the lowly. He has filled the hungry with good things, and the rich He has sent away empty" (verses 52, 53).

Jesus reflected this concept in His ministry. When the Pharisees observed Him eating with tax collectors and sinners He said, "Those who are well have no need of a physician, but those who are sick. . . . For I did not come to call the righteous, but sinners, to repentance" (Matt. 9:12).

Right up to the cross itself Jesus demonstrated this principle. God exalts the humble and blesses the needy. He turns failure into success, tragedy into triumph. When we are the most cognizant of our need, that is when His grace is most evident.

Good Tidings
of Great Joy

12

The Christian church at Corinth was having a bit of a squabble over, shall we say, evangelistic pedigree. Some had been brought into the church by Paul, others by Peter, and still others by Apollos. They were not arguing about doctrine—as far as we know, the instructions they had received had been the same, regardless of the preacher. It was the preachers they were arguing about. They were ranking the preachers and then ranking the members according to who had been converted by whom.

This was anathema to Paul. What difference did it make who had done the baptizing of anybody? The preachers were only instruments of Christ and His Spirit. It was to God they should look for instruction, for role model, for church leadership.

God's ways are not our ways. In fact, in just about any type of endeavor we are likely to find that God does things just in reverse to the way we would do them. In Creation, God began with water and dirt and flowers; humankind, His "crowning act," was last. But we put up a statue in the park and then landscape around it. To make a nation of Abraham's descendants, God sent them into Egypt for 400 years. We would have situated them in Canaan and expected them to develop there. God sent Moses into the wilderness for 40 years to unlearn what he had learned in the world's most advanced court.

This is not perverseness on God's part. He does not react to us—doing things differently just to be spiteful. Rather, it is a demonstration of Satan's tactics. His way is just the opposite of

God's. It is only when the opposite tack does not work that he tries to counterfeit the truth.

Humans boast about their highest building, their fastest plane, the richest person, the best athlete. God asks, "Who has despised the day of small things?" (Zech. 4:10). He used a rod in the hand of Moses to dumbfound Pharaoh, to split the Red Sea, to call water from a rock. He used a jawbone in the hand of Samson to begin the downfall of the Philistines, and a stone in the hand of David to rekindle Israel's faith.

So Paul tells the Corinthians that God is not interested in hierarchy. "Has not God made foolish the wisdom of this world?" (1 Cor. 1:20). "The foolishness of God is wiser than men, and the weakness of God is stronger than men. For you see your calling, brethren, that not many wise according to the flesh, not many mighty, not many noble, are called. But God has chosen the foolish things of the world to put to shame the wise, and God has chosen the weak things of the world to put to shame the things which are mighty; and the base things of the world and the things which are despised God has chosen, and the things which are not, to bring to nothing the things that are, *that no flesh should glory in His presence"* (verses 25-29).

" 'Not by might nor by power, but by my Spirit,' says the Lord of hosts" (Zech. 4:6). This is the way God works in the human heart. He does not force us, but tugs at us with the cords of kindness and love.

This principle was demonstrated again and again in the circumstances surrounding the Saviour's birth. No manifestation of power or force, no nod to human thirst for position or aggrandizement. God did not force Himself on Caesar or Herod, or even on the Sanhedrin. And He does not force His way into our hearts.

A simple maiden in a country town was chosen to be the mother of the Son of God. A carpenter was selected to be His foster father. A country priest fathered the one who was to proclaim the arrival of the King of heaven. And a stable was Jesus' home. Despise the day of small things, indeed! The Saviour of the world began His human sojourn in the humblest of surroundings, an Eastern stable.

And who were the first to receive the honor of an audience

with the infant King? Shepherds!

Surely there were more important people in Bethlehem the night the Lord was born! The tax decrees of Augustus knew no class lines among the Jews. There would be wealthy traders, land-holders, titled persons. There would be rulers of synagogues, mag-istrates, and governors. These classes, too, uprooted by the imperial decree, would have found themselves in the "city of David."

They would be in the inns, or staying with friends. Or they might have chosen to make their temporary abode in Jerusalem, only five miles away. They could find sumptuous quarters there, befitting their status. Why were not these people invited by Jesus' attending angel to the mangerside of Israel's Messiah?

For that matter, why were not the nation's rulers, who nor-mally lived in Jerusalem, summoned to Bethlehem? In Jerusalem were the high priest and his close entourage; there was the Sanhedrin, highest religious court. Herod had a palace there, with royal attendees. What an honor it would have been to be the first to welcome the world's Redeemer, the first to pledge allegiance to the divine Monarch!

But title, class, wealth, meant nothing when the heavenly mes-sengers sought to announce the holy birth. Past palace and man-sion, ignoring shopkeeper and politico alike, pausing not a moment with learned professors or distinguished scribes, the an-gels went to "shepherds living out in the fields" (Luke 2:8).

Shepherds represented one of the lowest classes of society in Israel. Not only were they poor, but also they were uneducated—social misfits. They didn't even attend regularly at the synagogue, and almost never took part in rites at the Temple. Unclean, that is what they were; not in the sense of lepers, but still outside the pale of respectable society—at least to the "society people" themselves.

Not that they had always been in such low esteem. Abraham had been a shepherd, and, of course, Isaac and Jacob. Moses had spent 40 years tending sheep, and even David spent his early years with the flock. Some of the prophets had been called from shep-herds' tasks to fill heavy responsibilities.

In one of His homilies Jesus described Himself as "the good shepherd." Then He enumerated the qualities that characterize a good shepherd. Such a one must put the welfare of the flock above his own—thus he must be dependable, responsible. He must be patient with his charges or he will lose them.

After nearly 30 years in the courts of Pharaoh, being groomed for the Egyptian throne, Moses was far from patient. In fact, he slew an Egyptian in a moment of hot anger. His 40 years with a flock mellowed him and prepared him to lead a cantankerous and obstinate people out of Egypt to Canaan.

This, then, is why the angels sought out shepherds to be the recipients of earth's gladdest tidings. They were humble, teachable. Unlike the haughty leaders of God's people, they were not jealous of their own power and position.

Perhaps most important of all, they sincerely anticipated the coming of the Messiah. They looked for the One who would release them from their burden of sin. God could speak to them, and they would listen.

And one more thing: They would take the good news to others. The religious leaders at the Temple had received a message about the imminence of the Messiah. Zacharias, one of their own, had received a vision right in the Temple itself. Zacharias told them about it: He would have a son who would herald the Promised One. And what did they do about it? Nothing! They didn't question Zacharias to get all the details. They didn't look up the prophecies to see what this meant. They didn't get the word out to the people that the great day was just a few months away.

The shepherds were "keeping watch over their flock by night" (verse 8). Literally, they were "watching watches"—not timepieces, but taking turns staying awake so that no harm would come to their flocks. They had often talked among themselves about the promise of the Messiah. They longed for the Holy One of Israel to come as promised. They knew that prophecy pinpointed their own little town of Bethlehem as His birthplace.

By analyzing the account of the shepherds, Bible students have tried to find some clue as to the time of year when Jesus was born. Noting that Palestinian winters are cold and wet, some conclude that the holy event must have occurred during the dry season, that is, between April and November. Otherwise, the sheep would have been put up in folds for protection.

But there is another angle for consideration. The Mishnah, a part of the Talmud, reports that near Bethlehem, on the road to Jerusalem, was a sheep tower called *Migdal 'Eder* ("tower of the flock"). This was a gathering place for those flocks destined for sacrifice at the Temple. (See *The SDA Bible Commentary,* vol. 5, p. 699). It will be remembered that sacrificial sheep must be carefully selected, without blemish. From this point near Bethlehem, they were taken at regular intervals into Jerusalem.

How ironic if this were the case—that the people who cared for the animals that would give their lives in type of the Lamb of God should be the first to worship Him in person!

But there is one item: These sacrificial flocks gathered at *Migdal 'Eder* all year round, not just in the dry season.

Enough speculation. Under the starry sky the sheep were asleep. Evening noises from the town had stilled. Only an occasional snore from a herdsman broke the solitude. Suddenly the countryside was bathed with light. It was enough to awaken the sleepers. An angel appeared in the radiance. The shepherds were "terrified" (verse 9, NIV).

"Do not be afraid," the angel encouraged, "for behold, I bring you good tidings of great joy which shall be to all people. For there is born to you this day in the city of David a Savior, who is Christ the Lord" (verses 10, 11).

Later in Jesus' ministry, when He was trying to establish a beachhead of faith, He was careful in declaring His divinity. He let His works speak for themselves, and many believed. But only toward the end did He openly avow Messiahship. But not so on this night, to these men of faith and rectitude. The Babe was Christ the Lord, plainly and positively. "Christ" is the Greek equivalent of the Hebrew "Messiah."

"Suddenly there was with the angel a multitude of the heavenly host praising God" (verse 13). The hills and skies were full of them. They had been there all the time, unseen, just bursting for the opportunity to exalt the Almighty for His marvelous gift to sinners. How considerate of them to hold off, to let just one angel approach the shepherds first. Had they all burst upon the poor men at once with their celebration, it could well have caused heart stoppage!

"Glory to God in the highest," the chorus sang, "and on earth peace, good will toward men!" (verse 14). This song has been translated variously. The New International Version reads, "peace to men on whom his favor rests."

Another possible rendering is "peace toward men of good-will." But that would seem to limit God's peace. The first angel had said that the tidings of joy that he bore was "to be to all people." "God so loved the world that He gave His only begotten Son, that *whoever* believes in Him should not perish but have everlasting life" (John 3:16). God extends peace even to those who are not of goodwill. He hopes that by His peace He can change their hearts so that they can be of goodwill. He calls not the righteous but sinners to repentance.

Although the initial announcement of Jesus' birth was made to lowly shepherds, the rich and the wealthy and the powerful are not left out of God's love. The Wise Men of the East were among His early admirers. Nicodemus and Joseph of Arimathea were later counted among His disciples. But how many were the shepherds and fishermen and tillers of the soil who loved Him!

If you are a person of means, let it not be a stumbling block to your faith. God loves you, too. Resolve to be a channel of blessing to others. If you are a person of humble circumstances, rejoice: "There is born to you . . . a Savior, who is Christ the Lord."

"Glory to God" and "peace to men." Doesn't that have a familiar ring? Jesus said the two great commandments are to love the Lord with all our heart and soul and to love our neighbors as ourselves. That is the essence of the Ten Commandments, the eternal principle of God's government.

As the angels faded from sight, the sound of their voices seemed to linger on the night air. But the shepherds did not linger. Following the instructions given, they made their way into town. They "came with haste" (Luke 2:16), looking for a stable, for a manger with a baby in it. We don't know how many stables they searched, how many people they woke up in their quest, but they were not to be denied until they found their Lord.

Perhaps they knew the couples of their town well enough to know which ones were expecting, and which of those had a stable. None of them? Then it would be a visiting couple. Bingo! They would go to the inn. (Nobody said these shepherds weren't smart!)

And what was going through Joseph's mind all this time?

With mother and Child resting, as they are wont to do after the rigors of childbirth, Joseph had opportunity for reflection. Did he wonder why there had been no communication from heaven since his dream? Was not the imminent birth of the Son of God important enough that he or his wife should be kept abreast of heaven's intentions and preparations? Why was not there some divine display as the most important Child on earth was born?

Not that Joseph once doubted the angel of his dream, or Mary's recital of her encounter with Gabriel. He was satisfied—nay, overjoyed—that her Child was the Saviour. But a little heavenly demonstration would have seemed appropriate.

If indeed Joseph harbored these thoughts, they were soon answered. Within a few hours after Mary had carefully bathed and wrapped her precious Baby, there arose a commotion at the door. Joseph opened it to a delegation of herdsmen, all breathless and starry eyed. No strangers to stables, the shepherds quickly explained their quest.

So heaven had taken note of the royal birth! That the display had been made to others was so much better than had it been limited to the stable room, with just Joseph and Mary as witnesses. The unusual birth was now a matter of public record.

The new parents must have had as many questions for the shepherds as the latter had for them. Everyone rejoiced in the marked culmination of their hopes—the fruition of dreams of thousands of generations before them. God had stepped into the stream of humanity, and the world would never be the same.

"Good news" is how the angel had described the message he had for the shepherds, and that is exactly what they thought of it. They were in as big a hurry to broadcast their good news as they had been to find the Baby. "They made widely known the saying which was told them concerning this Child" (verse 17).

The Greek word for "good news" is the same from which we get the word "evangelize." That is what those shepherds did throughout the town of Bethlehem, all the way back to their flocks. They could no more hold back from telling what they had seen, both in the fields and in the stable, than the angels could when Christ was born.

There is a place for the divine messenger, for visits from angels. There is also a place for dreams and visions as communications from God. But there is just as surely a place for the human witness in evangelism. When a flesh-and-blood representative of heaven—that is, you and I—shares the good news of the gospel, describing personal victory over temptation and appealing to the sin-burdened heart, there is a stronger influence than if the appeal is more subjective.

The Holy Spirit uses the compassion in our voice, the love in our eyes, the strength of our faith, to draw others to Christ. We can be examples of the worthwhileness of following Christ, an example of what God can do with a person. "There is nothing that the Saviour desires so much as agents who will represent to the world His Spirit and His character" *(The Acts of the Apostles*, p. 600).

Those shepherds were the first Christian evangelists. They told what they had seen and heard and felt. The stupendousness of the news they bore lent passion to their witness.

Today we have the same message. Pray that we may have the same passion.

Eternal Christmas

13

After creating Adam and Eve, God came often to the Garden of Eden to spend time with them, walking and visiting with them. But sin dropped a curtain between God and His creatures, the ones made in His own image. Surely God missed His association with them.

God took every opportunity to be with humans. He appeared to Abraham and had lunch with him and his wife, Sarah. He revealed Himself to Jacob more than once. He visited Moses and had a conversation with him on Mount Sinai. Moses' face glowed for a long time after that meeting.

The time came when God could not stand the separation any longer. He said to Moses, "I want you to build Me a sanctuary that I may *live with you.*" God took up residence in the completed sanctuary. The people of Israel could tell when He was "at home" in the middle of their camp by the pillar of cloud by day and fire by night that rested over the Most Holy Place.

Later God appeared to Joshua, at the edge of the Promised Land. He was seen with the three Hebrew exiles in Nebuchadnezzar's furnace.

But these were theophanies, God appearing as a man but not really one. He intended more: He would join the human race! He had told Eve that her Seed—a descendant of her very flesh, the fruit of a human womb—would be the one finally to destroy the destroyer, Satan.

Isaiah spoke of that One to come in the following words:

"Unto us a Child is born, unto us a Son is given; and the government will be upon His shoulder. And His name will be called Wonderful, Counselor, Mighty God, Everlasting Father, Prince of Peace" (Isa. 9:6).

Carefully God bided His time, waiting for the right conditions, both on earth and in the universe at large. More was at stake than just God's loneliness, or even our salvation. His government, His right to rule, was on the line.

Then "when the fullness of the time had come, God sent forth His Son, born of a woman, born under the law, to redeem those who were under the law, that we might receive the adoption as sons" (Gal. 4:4, 5).

What thoughts were in Jesus' mind "when the fullness of the time [was] come"? There was that last hour that He was to spend in heaven, the last few minutes He would have unimpeded fellowship with His Father, the last time that He would have "the form of God."

And now the time was at hand. In a few minutes the Son would lay aside all the prerogatives of God—the glory, the omnipotence, the omniscience. He would become a zygote, an embryo, a fetus, a baby in wet diapers. For nine months He would not know a thing. Then He would learn as any baby learns from his parents. He would be dependent upon the Holy Spirit to teach Him and to strengthen Him for His ordeal.

Before He left heaven Jesus knew of the confrontations He would have with the devil, in the devil's territory. He knew that Gethsemane would come, and after that, Golgotha. Jesus knew.

Did He experience the same trepidation you or I would experience under similar circumstances, on the brink of eternal consequences? No being had ever been in the situation He was going into. The fact that He as God could see into the future would not save Him from making a mistake—some horrible, unredeemable mistake—as a human on earth.

The minutes—if there are minutes in heaven—ticked away. The moment of truth arrived, and Jesus took that irrevocable step.

The pieces of prophecy were falling into place—the who, the what, the when. There remained only one piece—where. Micah had pinpointed Bethlehem of Judea: "But you, Bethlehem Ephrathah, though you are little among the thousands of Judah, yet out of you shall come forth to Me the One to be ruler in Israel, whose goings forth have been from of old, from everlasting" (Micah 5:2).

But Bethlehem was 75 miles—three days' journey, under good conditions—from Nazareth, where Joseph and Mary lived. And they were poor. They had no friends or relatives in Bethlehem with whom to stay while Mary filled her term. They could not afford to stay in an inn. Closer and closer the time came for Mary's delivery.

The matter was taken out of their hands by a decree from Rome. Everyone in the entire empire must return to his or her ancestral home and register in a census. The head count would be used as a basis for future military service and for taxation—except that the Jews were exempt from the military. Inasmuch as both Joseph and Mary were of David's line, they had to go to his hometown, Bethlehem. No allowance could be made for Mary's condition—they *had* to go, poor or no, and *now*.

Luke speaks of Mary as Joseph's betrothed wife, and some ancient manuscripts omit the word "wife." Yet Matthew says Joseph married Mary right after the angel told him to. More than likely, Luke was implying that they had not yet consummated their marriage sexually, which Matthew supports. Also, popular story has Mary riding on a donkey for the trip, but the Sacred Record does not give that detail. Perhaps she walked the whole way, and inasmuch as she was heavy with child, it may have taken them more than three days.

In any case, when they reached their destination, there was no place to stay. Thousands of other people were under the same orders as they. Probably most of the Jews at that time were descendants of Judah or Benjamin, the two tribes that made up the kingdom taken into Babylonian exile and later returned. All the towns and villages of Judea were crowded. With expatriate Jews from the Dispersion, Judea must have been one mass pandemonium. Under these circumstances, Joseph and Mary may have been fortunate to get accommodation in a stable!

Again, popular story has it that Mary gave birth that night, and again there is no confirmation in Scripture. However, the rigors of the trip she had taken likely would induce childbirth pretty quickly! Another reason we can assume Jesus was born that first night is that another day would have given them another chance to find other accommodations.

Did Joseph and Mary have assistance for the delivery, perhaps from the innkeeper's wife? Probably not, inasmuch as Mary herself "wrapped Him in swaddling cloths, and laid Him in a manger" (Luke 2:7).

Let's take a reality check now as we look at this Child. He is a human baby, as much human as you and I. "Inasmuch then as the children have partaken of flesh and blood, He Himself likewise shared in the same" (Heb. 2:14). John says "the Word [speaking of Jesus] became flesh and dwelt among us" (John 1:14).

The other reality as we look at this Babe in the manger is that He is very God. This "Word" (who became flesh) "was with God, and the Word was God" (verse 1). "For in him dwells all the fullness of the Godhead bodily" (Col. 2:9).

This Baby was the one who created the world: "All things were made through Him, and without Him nothing was made that was made" (John 1:3; see also Col. 1:16, 17). This One called "Christ" by the angels to the shepherds (Luke 2:11) was the Yahweh (Jehovah) of the Old Testament. He was the Rock who guided Israel through the wilderness (1 Cor. 10:4). It was His presence that Israel saw in the pillar of cloud and fire.

There was never a time that Jesus did not exist. "He was in the beginning with God" (John 1:2).

Right here perhaps we should take a moment to consider why Jesus was called the "Son of God," the "only begotten of the Father." If Jesus was equal with the Father, why is He spoken of as "begotten"? If He was never born, how could He be a Son?

The Greek word in John 1:14 and elsewhere in the New Testament that is translated "only begotten" is *monogenes,* which is properly translated "only one of a kind," "unique." Thus the New International Version has it, "the One and Only." Jesus does, indeed, share a unique relationship with the Father, but it has nothing to do with His origin! When we properly understand His Sonship, we will also understand His uniqueness.

Before the sin question arose, the three Beings who are one God shared identity, on a par with each other—one in purpose, one in method, one in motive. As They were about to create Adam

They said, "Let Us make man in Our image, according to Our likeness" (Gen. 1:26). How could one man be made in the image of three beings if They were different? But to meet the challenge of sin God held a council. One Member (we don't know what Their individual names were before the sin problem) volunteered to take a subordinate position to the others; He would become a human being and die as a human in atonement for the sins of humanity. Another Supreme Being would accept that atonement on behalf of the Godhead. The third member of the Godhead would serve as the dynamic in effecting the desired relationship between humans and God.

This is spelled out in Philippians 2:5-11: Christ Jesus, "who, being in very nature God, did not consider equality with God something to be grasped, but made himself nothing, taking the very nature of a servant, being made in human likeness" (verses 5-7, NIV).

Christ's subordination, His Sonship, was a matter of decision, not of origin. "I will declare the decree," the psalmist quotes Jesus as saying, "The Lord has said to Me, 'You are My Son, today I have begotten You'" (Ps. 2:7). That decision, that decree, met its reality when the Father raised the Son from the grave (see Acts 13:32, 33). In short, Jesus was Son by decree, not by generation.

In recognition that the eventuality was certain, the Father could speak of Jesus as His Son as early as Jesus' baptism. Jesus spoke of His Father even earlier, when His parents found Him in the Temple.

Back to Baby Jesus in a Bethlehem manger. He was all human and at the same time all divine. That was what made Him unique, the "One and Only." "For there is no other name under heaven given among men by which we must be saved" (Acts 4:12).

That Jesus is at once human and divine is what qualified Him to become our Saviour. As a human being He died for our sins. As the Source of life He gives us eternal life. Being at once man and God, He can take hold of our hand and at the same time take hold of the Father's hand and effect reconciliation—bring us together.

And as God-man, Jesus bears the name Immanuel, "God with us" (Matt. 1:23).

When He left heaven Jesus laid aside the attributes we generally associate with God—the glory, omnipotence, omniscience, omnipresence. What He did retain was His innate nature—His Godness. He took on humanity but kept His divinity.

Now note this: In taking human nature, Jesus took it for all time. When He returned to heaven after His resurrection, He reassumed many of the attributes He had held before (Heb. 1:1-4), but not all. He went back to heaven as a man (Luke 24:38-40), and He will return that way (Acts 1:11). Throughout eternity Jesus will retain His human body, along with the marks of His human suffering. If the essence of Christmas is "God with us," then in Christ we have eternal Christmas.

Very little of this did Mary comprehend as she gazed at her Child. She knew in her innermost soul that He was God, but it must have been impossible to always keep that in the forefront of her consciousness—He looked so human, He acted so human. And it was important that she treat Him as a human child. Then He would do something or someone would say something—the shepherds, for instance—that reminded her He was different, and she would ponder it in her heart (Luke 2:19).

As faithful and law-abiding Jews, Joseph and Mary were careful to follow all the Jewish mores as applied to their Son. On the eighth day He was circumcised, signifying His joining the covenant that bound Israel with their God. Thirty-two days later, the trio went into Jerusalem to the Temple. It was necessary for Mary to be ceremonially purified following childbirth, and this was a convenient time for the dedication of their Son, as required by Mosaic law. Had they lived some distance from Jerusalem, any priest could have accepted the dedication, and the purification could have been accomplished by surrogate at the Temple.

All firstborn males belonged to the Lord and were to be dedicated to Him. This practice followed the night in Egypt when Israel's firstborn were spared the death of the tenth plague. In the ceremony, the child was formally presented to the priest, who gave two short benedictions, and the parents paid a redemption price of five sanctuary shekels.

Purification of the mother consisted of two sacrifices. The sin offering was to be a turtledove or pigeon. The burnt offering, if the family could afford it, was to be a lamb; if not, a turtledove or pigeon could be offered. This was what Mary and Joseph brought.

Immediately after Mary's offering, an old man, Simeon, found the little family. He had been expressly informed by the Holy Spirit that he would not die until he had seen the Promised One. Now the Spirit directed him to the Temple, and pointed out to him the Baby.

Reverently Simeon took the child and held Him up before the Lord. Then he prayed, "Lord, now You are letting Your servant depart in peace, according to Your word; for my eyes have seen Your salvation which You have prepared before the face of all peoples, a light to bring revelation to the Gentiles, and the glory of Your people Israel" (Luke 2:29-32).

Interesting that Simeon should echo the words of the angel who appeared to the shepherds—this Jesus would be the salvation of *all* people, not just the Jews. Indeed, this was the promise made to Adam and Eve, as spoken to the serpent: "I will put enmity between you and the woman, and between your seed and her Seed" (Gen. 3:15). Jesus was the son of Eve, the mother of the human race, not just the son of Mary. It was in this sense that Jesus often referred to Himself as the Son of man. He came as the Saviour of the entire race.

Then Simeon addressed Mary: "Behold, this Child is destined for the fall and rising of many in Israel, . . . (yes, a sword will pierce through your own soul also)" (Luke 2:34, 35).

Just then another aged saint came up. Anna was a devout woman who spent her days in the precincts of the Temple, "with fastings and prayers night and day" (verse 37). She too recognized in the Infant the hope of glory. Not only did she praise God that she had seen the Saviour, but she also "spoke of Him to all those who looked for redemption in Jerusalem" (verse 38).

With all these manifestations of divine activity—Zacharias' vision right there in the Temple, the report of the shepherds, Simeon's and Anna's testimony—it boggles the mind that the spiritual leaders of Israel did not at least have an inkling of what was happening.

The little family returned to Bethlehem, where they had a house, rented, no doubt. Presumably Joseph had found customers for his carpentry trade. In fact, there is reason to believe that he did not intend to return to Nazareth. Had he wished to, he could have done so before now. But back there he could expect a lot of knowing looks and even some ungracious remarks about this Baby who had been conceived before the parents had been married. The Nazarenes were noted for saying what they thought.

Then one night—Jesus was perhaps a year old—there came more visitors, Magi, from the East. Their clothes and manner revealed their distinguished and wealthy position. They served their people in a priestly function. In their research they had come across prophecies about the appearance of a King among the Jews who would have special powers and influence far beyond Jewish borders. One of these prophecies was by Daniel, a man high in the Persian court. Another was by one of their own, Balaam. The latter had spoken of this King: "I see Him, but not now; I behold Him, but not near; a Star shall come out of Jacob; a Scepter shall rise out of Israel, and batter the brow of Moab, and destroy all the sons of tumult" (Num. 24:17).

Now, these Magi practiced a high degree of science, and one of their favorites was astronomy (some among them perverted their interests to astrology). When a strange star appeared in the western sky, they associated it with Daniel's time prophecy. So they determined to find out what was happening. It probably took them several months to mount their expedition, and then they lost more time in Jerusalem. But here they were, bearing expensive gifts.

The Magi did not linger. Their presence was a threat to the One they had come so far to worship. Herod was preparing his forces to eradicate this threat to his throne. They slipped away into the darkness. Joseph, too, warned of the danger, packed up his family and headed for Egypt. So soon were Simeon's words to Mary coming true.

How did those Magi recognize the Kingship of the infant Jesus? There was nothing about His physical appearance that would tell them. Surely it was the same power that had identified Him to Simeon and to Anna—the Holy Spirit. And here we need not be far behind them. The Spirit bears witness to our spirits, too, that Jesus is indeed the Christ, the anointed Son of God.

Let us worship!